Love + Log♡

Active Parenting of Teens

✓ *Web site*

Parent's Guide

by Michael H. Popkin, Ph.D.

ISBN 1-880283-19-0

Photography by Terry Cuffel.

In memory of

Bernard Howard
(1916 to 1989)

There are those who throw bricks through the dreams of others and those who provide bricks for others to build their dreams. Bernie Howard was a dream builder. Whenever someone came to him with an earnest dream that could help others, his position was always, "How can I help?" Whether it was providing dignified care for the elderly, shelter for the homeless, or a new approach to parent education, Bernie Howard reached for his checkbook when others reached for the door. When his advice was needed for writing a business plan or planning a building project, he was never too busy. He was there.

His contribution to the founding of Active Parenting Publishers is remembered in this dedication. May his memory live as long as caring people continue to support those who care about children and teens.

Michael H. Popkin, Ph.D., author
of Active Parenting of Teens

Introduction

"We are all here because we are scared to death about what our children will do when they become teenagers." These words, spoken by a father in a parenting group that I led more than fifteen years ago, still echo in my ears. We were dealing with parenting issues that related to five-year-olds, and yet the parents' motivation for learning was fear of the teen years.

And why not? The statistics on teen drug use, pregnancy, delinquency, and even suicide are enough to give any concerned parent pause for reflection. Am I doing all that I can to prepare my teen to face these dangers? Although we can never guarantee our children's success, we want to know in our hearts that we have given them our best efforts.

Part of giving our best means tackling the job of parenting like we would any other job that is both important and difficult—with training and support. For too long, however, our society has treated parenting as if it were either easy or unimportant, and parents have had to fend for themselves. Without training, families often experience frustration and conflict, and they're left wondering what went wrong.

Fortunately, there are answers. Parents and parent-education professionals have learned a lot over the years about what works and what doesn't work with teenagers. They have partnered with institutions that serve families to offer parent-education programs such as *Active Parenting of Teens*. They've committed themselves to make a difference.

When I founded Active Parenting Publishers in 1980, I was working as a child and family therapist. Part of my job was to provide counseling and therapy to individuals and families, and the other part was to provide parent-education courses and school consultation in the community. Over the years, I experienced firsthand the power effective parenting methods have to change the lives of parents and children. I saw unmotivated and unruly teenagers respond positively when their parents began to use these methods. I saw parents who had grown angry and distant "reawaken the feeling of love for my children," as one mother so poetically said.

Motivated by the knowledge that I had the right approach to parenting, I set out to develop a delivery system that would make these skills come alive for parents—one that would demonstrate these methods and make them easier to learn. The result was the original *Active Parenting Discussion Program*, the world's first video-based, parent-education program. The response was beyond my imagination as Active Parenting courses began to spring up throughout North America.

Since then, the original program has been replaced by three new programs: *1, 2, 3, 4 Parents!* (for parents of 1- to 4-year-olds), *Active Parenting Today* (for parents of 2- to 12-year-olds), and *Active Parenting of Teens* (for parents of teens and preteens). To date more than two million parents have completed at least one of these courses, with millions of others having experienced the all-video versions of the programs on television. These courses so far have been translated into five foreign languages and are now used in countries all over the world.

This book contains all the information and practical skills from the program. Some of these methods will take time to implement, but this investment of yourself now will save you and your family much time, frustration, and heartache later.

This book is your parenting resource. However, some of what you will read may not fit your own view of parenting. I hope you will keep an open mind and consider these ideas fairly. In the final analysis, you are the authority in your family. Feel free to pick and choose from this program what feels right to you, or, as one parent so aptly put it, "Use the best and let go of the rest."

I wish the best for you and your family.

Michael H. Popkin, Ph.D.

Table of Contents

Chapter 4: Responsibility and Discipline 132

Chapter 5: Cooperation and Communication 178

Chapter 6: The Problem-Solving Family in Action . . 212

Appendixes

The Active Parent

Parenting Teens Today

I recently took my family to visit the Kennedy Space Center in Cape Canaveral, Florida. Standing in the shadow of the giant Saturn rocket, I reflected on how awestruck I had been as a teenager watching the Mercury launches, the astronauts who risked their lives, and the ultimate triumph of putting human beings on the moon. What a challenge! What a victory for humankind! And as I appreciated what those heroes of science and technology had accomplished, I had an ironic thought: "Wouldn't it be great if parenting teens were as easy as putting a person on the moon?"

"Houston, we have a problem."

The world today is tough on teenagers. First and foremost, it's a dangerous place to raise them. Violence against teens—often by other teens—is so rampant that in many schools teens are afraid to go to the restroom for fear of being harassed, extorted, injured, or worse.

Substance abuse continues to plague teenagers in our neighborhoods and throughout the world, as more and more teens succumb to the temptation and pressure to use drugs. Many become overdose victims, addicts, car crash statistics, school drop-outs, and other casualties of the drug culture.

Our society, with its in-your-face media style, bombards teens with messages about sexuality and appearance that leave more than a million teenage girls pregnant each year and thousands suffering from eating disorders such as bulimia (bingeing and purging) and anorexia (self-starvation). Thousands of teens contract the fatal HIV virus annually. Many more have sex but have no idea how to have a respectful, loving relationship.

Today's teens struggle more than ever with their emerging sexuality.

Teens today are maturing faster than ever, with the average age of puberty dropping with each new generation. Many eleven-year-old girls are now young women biologically yet still children emotionally. By fifteen or sixteen, teens have been teens for so long that they often lose patience with adult rules and expectations. Yet they are going through so much change—physical, emotional, social, and intellectual—that they still need adult supervision and support.

Teens today are more likely than ever before to have parents who are divorced. Many live in single-parent homes, where financial pressure and inadequate supervision are common problems. Others have to deal with their parents' remarriages and their conflicting emotions at the introduction of new stepparents and perhaps new siblings to their lives.

More teens live in two-career families than ever before. Although this trend is positive in many ways, parental support and supervision—vital for these growing young people—is often lacking when both parents work. In one study, parents in dual-career families spent an average of five minutes a week with their teens!

The demands of an increasingly technological society mean that an

For many teenagers, these years are filled with pain, depression, even thoughts of suicide.

education is more important than ever, yet teens are dropping out of high school in record numbers, and many of those who stay graduate without really learning the fundamentals of reading and math. Others go on to college but have no sense of the value and requirements of work. They flounder from job to job, unsatisfied and unproductive.

Half a million teenagers attempt suicide each year. The fact that 5,000 actually die in this tragic way suggests that most kids are not really ready to give up . . . but they are crying for help.

The Good News

Although teens are more complex than rocket boosters and laws of physics, we have nevertheless learned a lot about the "guidance systems" that parents of teens need. This book will present a model for understanding and guiding teens that I developed more than a decade ago and that has been used effectively by more than a million and a half parents since then. It is called Active Parenting, for reasons that will become clear as you continue to read. The fact is that many families today not only help their children survive the dangerous teen years, but give them the resources that enable them to go on and thrive. With the support of knowledgeable and caring parents and other adults, many teens do well at school and at home, plus find time for sports, volunteer work, and other worthwhile interests. Yes, these teens and their families still have problems—no family gets through the teen years without some lost sleep. But they also have the skills and support to manage their problems effectively before they escalate out of control.

Teens in these families receive many of the same negative messages from society that their more troubled peers do, but their parents have learned how to help them separate the positive values from the negative. These parents have learned how to listen to their teens in ways that promote respectful two-way communication. They have learned how to support their teens in solving problems. And they have learned effective methods of discipline that help their teens grow into responsible young adults.

It is true that parenting is not the only influence on a teen's development. But it is the influence we can do the most about. *Active Parenting of Teens* is based on a combination of theory, research, and practical experience that is designed to help you maximize your ability to influence your teens in a positive direction. It will help you solve many of the daily hassles of family living and improve the overall relationship that you share with your children. Even more importantly, it will help you prepare your teens to become independent adults who have the skills and values to live fulfilling lives and make real contributions to their communities. And, if you approach the ideas presented here with an open mind, you will find ways of making these some of the best years your family has ever experienced.

The Tasks of Adolescence

The first step in helping your teens through these turbulent years is to learn something about what makes them tick. Psychological research over the last half century has taught us that all teens have certain "tasks" they are trying to accomplish—often subconsciously—as they mature towards full adulthood. These developmental tasks include:

- developing an identity independent of their parents in order to break away from them and then to return as their parents' peers.
- developing a philosophy of life and a value system upon which to make decisions.
- coming to terms with the need to work.
- coming to terms with their emerging sexuality.

Completing these developmental tasks in our stressful modern society is a major challenge for all teenagers. Add to this challenge the complications caused by major hormonal changes and rapid physical growth, and it's no wonder that teens often act like they are on an emotional roller coaster. One minute they may be loving children snuggling next to you on the sofa, and the next, raging aliens upset because you won't let them use the car. Regardless, one thing remains constant: They need you to help guide and support them through this difficult time.

Above all, your teen needs your love and support during these years of major physical and emotional change.

Teen Development

Do your teens do things that seem designed to drive you crazy? A lot of problematic teen behavior is rooted in struggles that all teens go through as part of the normal developmental process. Often this behavior is not a personal attack against parents (although it can seem like it is!).

Which of these characteristics are at the root of particular problems your teen is experiencing?

Developmental Characteristics ➝ Possible Behavior that Results

Pre-Teens

Developmental Characteristics	Possible Behavior that Results
Reproductive maturity reached: for girls, ages $8\frac{1}{2}$ to 13; for boys, ages $9\frac{1}{2}$ to 15	The beginning of sexual experimentation
Growing sense of independence and self-sufficiency	Starting to stray from family
Develop same-sex friendships and learn new social skills	May become very close to a best friend to the exclusion of family
Develop more concrete logic skills	May use jokes that seem cruel to vent aggression

Young Teens (approx. 12 to 14 yrs.)

Developmental Characteristics	Possible Behavior that Results
Rapid cycling through moods	Unpredictable and challenging behavior
Identity exploration begins	Experimentation with personality, peers, and appearance
Beginning concern with others' thoughts about them	General defensiveness due to strong feelings of self-consciousness
Developing capacity for critical analysis	Constant analysis and critique of family members
May believe they're invincible	Will reject warnings about health and safety issues from adults

Older Teens (approx. 15 to 18 yrs.)

Developmental Characteristics	Possible Behavior that Results
Complete physical development	Struggle to integrate natural sexual and emotional needs with society's messages and their own values Struggle to react appropriately to being treated as an adult
Develop the ability to think abstractly	May use irony and other sophisticated forms of humor to critique society
Capable of identifying with other people's conditions	Become more concerned about the feelings of others
Able to imagine the world as it should be and compare it to the way it is now	May become interested in making a difference in the world

Is This Your Teen?

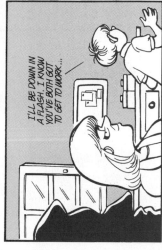

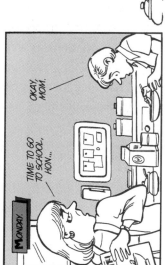

What is Active Parenting?

This family is using an "active" approach to parenting by communicating together to solve problems.

The approach to parenting presented in this book is called "active" in contrast to what parents often do, which might be called "reactive." "Reactive parenting" is characterized by waiting until teens push parents to their limits, and then reacting with random discipline. This parenting style is usually fraught with frustration, anger, and escalating conflict. Reactive parenting unwittingly allows teens to control situations as well as parents' emotions. Instead of preventing or solving problems, reactive parenting allows problems to continue, or even get worse, as parents and teens replay the same painful situations over and over.

The philosophy of Active Parenting of Teens *is that it is the job of the parent to play the leadership role in the family.* However, this is not a simple matter of laying down the law. Effective leadership in any organization, from a business to a family, is a matter of the right attitudes and skills.

The philosophy of *Active Parenting of Teens* is that it is the job of the parent to play the leadership role in the family.

It involves:

- anticipating and preventing problems pro-actively.
- developing mutually respectful relationships.
- enforcing fair discipline.
- maintaining effective communication.
- using productive problem-solving methods.
- encouraging the participation of everyone involved.

This book will cover these skills and other parenting methods that I have adapted from the work of great psychologists such as Alfred Adler and Rudolf Dreikurs and organized into the Active Parenting method. Over the past two decades, tens of thousands of parents have told me that the skills they learned in Active Parenting classes and books have not only made them more effective parents but have also made them more effective siblings, employees, and friends.

While I firmly believe that using the Active Parenting model of parenting will help improve relationships in your family, do not expect change overnight. It will take a little practice and time. Remember, we all make mistakes. First, we all make mistakes when learning new skills. Don't be too hard on yourself. Catch your mistakes with a smile, not a kick. Encourage yourself for trying and see what you can do differently next time. After all, mistakes are for learning. Second, you'll recognize mistakes you have made in the past and mistakes your own parents made with you. It is helpful to recognize these mistakes because, again, you can learn from them. But it is important to let go of negative feelings such as guilt and anger and use that energy to improve your own parenting now. If you have trouble letting go of such feelings on your own, sometimes individual or family counseling can be a great help.

The Purpose of Parenting

Though society has become more stressful for teens and parents, the basic purpose of parenting has not changed. We can state it like this:

The purpose of parenting is to protect and prepare our children and teens to survive and thrive in the kind of society in which they will live.

The dangers present in our modern society make it difficult to achieve the two goals of protection and preparation. We want to protect our teens so that they will survive. Yet if we protect them too much (overprotect them), we fail to prepare them to thrive on their own. Keep in mind that one of the objectives of parenting is to gradually work yourself out of a job!

What do you want for your teens?

Consider . . . the *Vasa*. In 1628 the Swedish battleship *Vasa* was emerging from the Stockholm harbor on its maiden voyage when it hit a storm, rolled over, and sank. The problem wasn't so much the storm—after all, other ships had withstood far worse storms. The problem was that the *Vasa* didn't have enough weight in its hull (ballast) to stabilize itself. Lacking the proper ballast, the *Vasa* was no match for the storm's winds and waves. It simply got knocked over and went down like a rock.

Teens in today's world are also traveling in dangerous waters. What will help protect our children when they are offered drugs? How can we help them when they are put into a physically dangerous situation, tempted to act out sexually, or come face to face with a host of other storms on the sea of adolescence? What will help them is the same thing that would have helped the *Vasa*: ballast—stabilizing weight at the teen's center. Ballast is also defined as "that which gives stability to character." It's the core values that you can help instill in your teens—the stable character they will need to make good decisions when the waves get high and the winds blow hard.

What values and qualities of character are important for your teens to develop?

The answer goes back to our purpose of parenting. If we are to protect and prepare our teens to survive and thrive in the kind of society in which they will live, we have to ask ourselves what it takes to survive and thrive in a democracy. Do we want people who will unquestioningly do as they're told, who are blindly obedient and fearful of authority? That might be useful if we were raising our teens to live under a dictatorship, but such qualities would not lead to success in a democratic society in which teens need to learn responsibility. Do we want teens who make their own rules and do as they want? This might be useful if they lived in a lawless society, but in our society of laws, such teens could end up in prison—or dead.

There are many qualities of character that are important for surviving and thriving in a democratic society, but four seem to form the foundation upon which other qualities build.

Courage

A free society provides many opportunities for people to succeed, but success is not easy. Those who have the confidence to take worthwhile risks have the best chance to thrive. And when life gets tough, those with the courage to persevere eventually succeed.

Among teenagers, it takes great courage to resist peer pressure. From the French word *coeur*, meaning heart, courage is the ballast that can stabilize your teen in a storm. We will focus on ways of instilling this fundamental quality in Chapter 2.

Responsibility

Responsibility—a crucial concept in parenting—is the ability to recognize one's obligations, to know right from wrong, and to accept the consequences of one's decisions.

Teens who learn to take responsibility for their choices by experiencing the consequences that follow eventually learn to make better choices. Many of the choices your teens have to make will affect their entire lives. They will be offered tobacco, alcohol, and other drugs, and they will choose to accept or decline. They will face choices about sex, about dropping out of school, about work and careers, and even about whether to commit crime. You won't be there, telling them what to do. But if you have prepared them to make responsible decisions and have instilled in them the courage to stand behind those decisions, they will be prepared to meet their challenges. We will explore methods of teaching responsibility throughout this book, and especially in Chapter 4.

Cooperation

It is the teen who learns to live and work cooperatively with others, not the lone wolf, who has the best chance to succeed. Democracy is based on the notion that "none of us is as smart as all of us." Competition has its role in our society, too, but the individual who values teamwork is one who moves society forward.

Learning cooperation skills begins in the family. Cooperation is fostered through everyday problem-solving and planning, which require effective communication and a spirit of mutual respect and participation. In Chapters 5 and 6 we will present communication skills that will help you win the cooperation of your teens while teaching them to solve problems and make decisions cooperatively with others. And in every chapter, we will present a "Family Enrichment Activity" to help you strengthen the relationship between you and your children.

Self-Esteem

High self-esteem will help your teen develop other qualities that lead to success.

Teens who believe they are worthwhile human beings, with talents and dreams that are worthy of respect, have the best chance of thriving. In fact, high self-esteem helps a person develop the courage, responsibility, and cooperation needed to succeed. At the same time, seeing oneself as someone who has such positive qualities as courage, responsibility, and cooperation builds higher self-esteem.

We will explore this cycle further in Chapter 2, as we look at how to help build a self-esteem in teens that is based on positive attitudes and actions, not self-hype.

Of course, you will want to encourage additional values and qualities of character in your teens. The skills you learn here will prove effective for encouraging whatever values are important in your family. Of more immediate concern, these skills will also work to reduce the conflicts and hassles of everyday living with teenagers.

Media–Driven Values

Helping our teens choose solid values in a culture based on short-term pleasures instead of long-term satisfaction is not an easy task. Movies, television, advertisements, music, and other cultural influences often portray self-destructive attitudes and behaviors in a positive light. Smoking, drinking, and even drug abuse and violence can appear cool when presented as entertainment or advertising. Teaching our teens the values of responsibility, cooperation, courage, respect, and self-denial ("I want to go with the kids to the game, but I really need to stay home and study") can seem dull by comparison. But these are some of the values that build long-term satisfaction. These lessons can help keep teens out of trouble and focused on success.

Styles of Parenting

Here is an important principle of leadership: *Leaders in a democratic society get their authority from those they lead.* The same is true for parents. We are the authorities in our families. But to be effective, we must have the cooperation of our children. Which leadership styles will foster this cooperation?

Leaders in a democratic society get their authority from those they lead.

As you read about the three parenting styles described here, keep in mind that most parents choose a particular parenting style because they honestly believe it is in their children's best interests. In fact, each does have some positive aspects. The key is to "keep the best and let go of the rest." As you begin to see yourself in some of these descriptions, you may conclude that you do not use any one style exclusively. As your parenting methods become clearer to you throughout this book, you will develop the knowledge and skills to be more consistent.

1. The Autocratic Style: The Dictator

The autocratic parent tries to be all-powerful in directing the lives of his children. This parent is a dominating, authoritarian figure who uses reward and punishment as tools to enforce his orders.

Finger-pointing and an angry posture are clear signs of an autocratic parenting style.

Teens are kept in line by the threat of punishment if they misbehave and the promise of reward if they do what parents wish them to do. Teens are told what to do, how to do it, and where to do it. There is little or no room for them to question, challenge, or disagree.

Children brought up in autocratic families seldom thrive. Sometimes their spirits are broken and they give up. More often, they rebel. This rebellion can be characterized by sneaking or by open defiance. Rebellion usually happens during teen years because the child has developed enough power to fight back. Autocratic parenting has been the typical parenting style for so many generations that teenage rebellion has come to be accepted by many experts as "normal." This is a mistake. Teenagers, as we will see, do not have to rebel to become independent.

The autocratic style of parenting can be described as "limits without freedom," and depicted as a closed circle. It worked reasonably well when inequality was the norm in social interactions, but it works poorly in today's world of increased equality. The autocratic parent deserves some credit for recognizing the need for limits and having the emotional strength to stand firm. But he goes much too far.

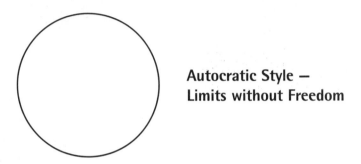

**Autocratic Style —
Limits without Freedom**

You are tending toward the autocratic style of parenting when you say things like:

- "Because I'm the parent and I said so!"
- "As long as you live under my roof, you'll obey my rules."
- "When you are the parent, you can decide what to do."

and when you do things like:

- tell your teen what to wear
- find yourself angry and yelling often
- ground or punish your teen in other ways often.

(2.) The Permissive Style: the Doormat

Permissive parents react strongly against the harsh and uncompromising autocratic method. Instead, they allow their teens to "do their own thing." In such households there is little respect for order and routine, and few limits are placed on anyone's freedom. Teens often have no curfew and few household responsibilities. They are pampered and accustomed to getting their own way. Permissive parents are like doormats, allowing their teens to walk all over them. Ironically, teens themselves do not feel happy in such an environment. Without a clear authority figure to protect them, teenagers feel insecure. They sometimes lose their sense of belonging with the family. Because they have not learned to understand others' needs and viewpoints, they are often difficult to live with.

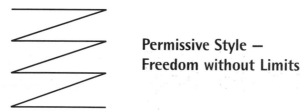

Permissive Style — Freedom without Limits

Teenagers from permissive homes often rebel or refuse to comply. Teens used to a lifestyle with no limits have trouble keeping a job. They also struggle with the healthy "give and take" of close relationships as they grow into adulthood.

The permissive method can be described as "freedom without limits," and shown as a squiggly line, meaning freedom run rampant. Although it is commendable that permissive parents understand the need for freedom and are willing to share power with their children, they go too far also.

You are tending toward the permissive parenting style when you say things like:

- "I don't think that's a good idea . . . but, well . . . okay, if you really want to."
- "Do you really need this? Oh, all right. Here's the money."
- "I sure wish you'd help out around here."

and when you do things like:

- ignore your teen's schoolwork until you see his low grades
- routinely do his homework with him or go to school to intervene for him often
- give in to her unreasonable demands because you're afraid she will become angry or sad.

3. The Authoritative Style: the Active Parent

In some respects, the Active Parenting style is the middle ground between the autocratic method and permissive method. It is also much more. In an active household, freedom is important, but so are the rights of others and one's own responsibilities. This parent encourages order and routine and understands the need for reasonable limits to behavior. The Active Parenting method acknowledges modern social equality and concentrates on the rights and responsibilities of all.

**Active Style —
Freedom within Expanding
Limits**

The active method could be called "freedom within expanding limits" and shown as a squiggly line within the limits of a circle. As the teen grows up and assumes more responsibility, the authoritative parent gradually relaxes limits until the teenager (at eighteen- to twenty-one-years-old) has the same amount of independence as an adult. This is what is meant by expanding limits.

The "active" style is a more respectful approach to parenting: Both teen and parent have a say in the issue.

Active Parenting acknowledges our democratic heritage and the role of social equality among all human beings in two important ways:

• Teens are treated with dignity and respect, even when their parents discipline them.

• Teens are entitled to express their thoughts and feelings, respectfully, to their parents. In this way they are given the right to influence the decisions that affect their lives. This is consistent with life in a democratic country, where you may not always get your way, but you always get your say.

You are tending toward the active style of parenting when you say things like:

• "I know you're dissappointed, but you can't go. Here's why . . ."
• "Sure we can talk about it. What's your idea?"
• "I know you can handle it. But if you need some help, just let me know."

and do things like:

• involve your teens in deciding who will do which family chores
• give her the full responsibility of her homework, monitoring her just a little

- show an active interest in her education by discussing her subjects with her regularly and attending school functions
- involve her in the discipline process by talking with her about your expectations and the consequences for breaking agreements
- letting him know what you like about him and encouraging him often
- talking with him about topics—such as drugs use, sexuality, and violence—in a calm and non-judgemental manner.

A Change of Perspective

If you think and act like an active parent, you'll find that you and your teen's relationship improves in surprising ways.

The best way to ensure a change in your teen's attitudes and behavior is by changing your own.

The following sections will get you started thinking like an active parent.

Why Reward and Punishment Often Backfire

I mentioned earlier that reward and punishment are tools that the autocratic parent uses to enforce her orders. This system of reward and punishment is sometimes effective in an autocratic environment, but in a society of equals it often makes matters worse.

For one thing, teens in these households eventually regard rewards for positive behavior almost as a right. If rewards are to be effective as incentives for continued positive behavior, parents often must increase the value of the reward until they reach a kind of bankruptcy. This bankruptcy often leads to the use of punishment. Punishment is not effective in the long run because it often leads teens to resent parents and to try to get even with them. It doesn't teach them how to behave—it teaches them only how to effectively coerce or hurt someone.

In fact there is no place for reward and punishment between people who respect each other. All in all, reward and punishment as methods of discipline are holdovers from an earlier time when the world was a different place. Parents can employ much more effective methods of discipline, and you will read about those methods in this book, particularly in Chapter 4.

Control versus Influence

We have all heard people talk about how important it is for parents to control their teens. The truth is that the only person who can really *control* a teen's behavior is the teen himself. Our strength lies in *influencing* our teen's behavior and attitude. What's the difference?

Control means you have 100% power over the outcome.

Influence means you have between 1 and 99 percent power over the outcome.

If you tend towards the autocratic style, you probably try to over-control your teen. Ironically, often the more control you try to exert, the more your teen rebels against your authority. The result is that other influences, from peers to the media, gain the remaining influence. If you are more of an active parent, you work hard at being a positive influence in your teen's life, using a combination of respectful discipline and support. Even so, recognize that your influence can ultimately go only so far. Teens have free will and make the final decisions about their attitudes and behavior.

As important a role as we play in our teen's development, we can never take full credit or blame for the outcome. Many highly loving and effective parents have had teens make bad decisions and fail to thrive, or even survive. On the other hand, many parents who were neglectful or even abusive have had teens survive and thrive in spite of their negative influence. Parenting is really about probabilities. We improve the probability that our teens will succeed by being the best influence we can be. And we encourage them to be around others who will be positive influences as well.

The Method of Choice

All parents sometimes want their children to do something. Often, all the parent has to do is ask for what she wants respectfully, and the teen complies.

Example:

Parent: Please put away those comics and start your homework.

Teen: Okay.

Also often, the teen doesn't like to be told what to do, and it goes like this:

Example:

Parent:	Please put away those comics and start your homework.
Teen:	I'll do it later.
Parent:	You need to do your homework. Now put down those comics and get started.
Teen:	I don't see why I can't do it later.
Parent:	That's what you always say, but it doesn't get done! Now get in there and start your homework now!
Teen:	That's not fair!

Offering your teen a choice, instead of dictating to her, can head off many power struggles.

When teens feel that their parents are trying to control them, they often rebel. The result is a power struggle that leaves both parent and teen frustrated and angry. A simple method to head off many of these power struggles is to provide the teen with a choice, instead of an order. The choice should be within the limits that you think are reasonable for the situation. This is the heart of "freedom within limits," which is the hallmark of life in a democracy, as well as the active style of parenting.

Example:

Parent:	I think we need to set a regular time for you to do your homework; that way I won't be nagging you all the time.
Teen:	Ah . . . mom.
Parent:	Would you rather do it before dinner or after?

Teen: After, I guess.

Parent: Okay. Right after dinner, then.

Teen: Okay.

Choice is power. *When you give a teen a choice you give him legitimate power. When you give him an order, he will have to rebel to gain power.* As leader in the family, give your teens choices that are appropriate for their ages and levels of responsibility. Sometimes these choices might be simple either/or choices, as in the above example. Other times you might give open-ended choices.

When you give a teen a choice you give him legitimate power. When you give him an order, he will have to rebel to gain power.

Example:

"Remember, you're going to cook dinner tomorrow. What would you like me to pick up at the grocery store when I'm there?"

"We would like to visit Grandma pretty soon. What's a good weekend for you?"

When we start thinking in terms of choices, instead of dictating to them or giving in, we begin to move from power struggles to problem-solving. Finding solutions that are acceptable to both of you is also a good way to prepare your teen to be a good decision-maker. The ability to make good decisions is critical when teenagers are confronted with choices about drugs, sexuality, and violence.

One word of caution: Don't make everything a choice. Many times teens just want a clear but friendly decision from a parent.

Method of Choice Practice Sheet

Choices to give my teen this week:

Teen's name:_____

Choice:_____

How did it go?_____

_____

Teen's name:_____

Choice:_____

How did it go?_____

_____

Teen's name:_____

Choice:_____

How did it go?_____

_____

Teen's name:_____

Choice:_____

How did it go?_____

_____

Teen's name:_____

Choice:_____

How did it go?_____

_____

Teen's name:_____

Choice:_____

How did it go?_____

Ethnic Identity Development

If your teen belongs to a minority ethnic group, she may grapple with new emotions and awareness in addition to the changes all teens experience.

When children are young, they are aware of simple racial differences—skin color, for example—but not of the significance society assigns to these differences. As they grow into teens and have more opportunities for social contact, they begin to observe, make comparisons, and evaluate society's fairness. Often this increasing awareness has a predictable set of stages:

1. **Conforming:** This is a naive acceptance of the dominant culture's values. At this stage, your child or young teen may put down her own family's culture while idealizing the dominant culture.

2. **Questioning/Thinking:** Your teen may begin to wonder why some people accept the dominant culture without complaint. She may show a growing interest in her own cultural heritage.

3. **Resisting:** A teen at this stage will show interest and pride in her own culture only and will reject the dominant culture's values. She will resist dominance by the cultural and political majority.

4. **Awareness:** At this stage the teen will think more critically about her own culture, while still maintaining pride. She will accept certain aspects of the dominant culture, even as she continues to resist conforming to the mainstream.

You can gently guide your teen through these stages with support, understanding, and lots of discussion. Encourage your child to learn about her ethnic history. Teens want to learn, and they want to know that you care about their feelings. Your support, not your resistance, will help your teen through this challenging time.

Spending time together learning about your ethnic history can be enriching for both of you.

Drugs, Sexuality, and Violence: Storms at Sea

On Saturday afternoon, thirteen-year-old David met up with some buddies to play basketball. On the way to the blacktop, one of them pulled out a brown paper bag, unscrewed the top of the bottle inside, and took a short swig of 80 proof whiskey. Without a word he passed the bottle to the guy next to him, who took a swig. As the bottle moved from teen to teen, the pressure on David mounted. He didn't want to drink, but he didn't want to look like a kid either. And he didn't want to be left out of the group.

At an unsupervised party on Saturday night at 11:30, James, seventeen, had already had six beers and was well on the way to "getting totally wasted" for the third time this month. His girlfriend, Selena, was drinking almost as heavily and beginning to enjoy the attention of Joey, one of the other guys at the party. James was furious. He started shouting and shoving Joey before some of the others separated the two boys. James left the party with Selena, cursing and yelling at her while they drove home for being "such a slut." Selena yelled back. As they pulled into her driveway, James slapped her hard across the face and told her to "shut up."

At the same party, just after midnight, fifteen-year-old Dawn was losing her virginity in an upstairs bedroom with Keith, a boy she had known only a few weeks. Though not drunk, both had been drinking and taking turns smoking a joint. Dawn would later describe the experience as "nothing like I expected. It wasn't romantic at all and it hurt real bad. I was glad when it was over."

Drinking lowers inhibitions for teens, which can lead to other drug use, risky sexual behavior, or violence.

Do these scenarios shock you? Sadly, they are not extreme or even uncommon experiences among today's teens. Of all the challenges facing today's teens, the three most threatening are probably drugs, sexuality, and violence. Each of these dangers not only has the potential to hurt a teen's life, it can also end that life. Many teenagers compound the risk factor by sailing into all three storms at once. As the stories above suggest, a teen high on alcohol or other drugs is many times more likely to become sexually active and/or physically violent.

Parents can do much to help prevent tragedy in these areas. First, the skills you learn in this book will help you build a positive relationship with your teens. Offering choices is the first step to empowering your teens, letting them know you trust them to make a decision. Building a positive relationship with your teens will increase your ability to influence them to make good decisions about drugs, sexuality, and violence. It will also decrease the likelihood of them making bad decisions just to get back at you for being a dictator or a doormat.

Second, by helping your teens develop courage, self-esteem, responsibility, cooperation, and other important qualities, you help them achieve the stability of character, or ballast, needed to make it through adolescent storms and continue on to become successful adults.

Third, you can use concrete prevention strategies to directly reduce the chances of your teens becoming harmfully involved with alcohol and other drugs, with sexuality, and with violence. These strategies are based on the findings of a task force I served on for the U.S. Office of Substance Abuse Prevention (OSAP). I have slightly modified these ten strategies to apply to sexuality and violence as well as drugs. These strategies will be presented throughout the book in this section of each chapter.

Our Philosophy

Drugs, sexuality, and violence issues evoke controversy. People take different stands on abortion, sex before marriage, sexual orientation, the use of alcohol and drugs such as marijuana, and when to fight and when to walk away. It is not my purpose to tell you what stand to take on these and other controversial issues. Instead, sections throughout this book will provide you with the information and skills to help you instill in your teenagers the values important in your family. *Please understand that you will not always succeed.* Your children will adopt some beliefs that will be different from yours, perhaps on very important issues. You may be tempted to fight this—to reject your teens' beliefs, and by extension, them. If you do, you will lose the opportunity to be an influence in other areas of their lives as well. Worse, you will have renounced your responsibility as a parent.

We may not always understand our teens, but we can always love them and offer support and discipline as needed.

Active Parenting's philosophy is to accept our children, even when we reject their values or their behavior. *We may not always understand them, but we can always love them and offer support and discipline as needed.*

A Scary Picture

The statistics underscoring the problems related to drugs, sexuality, and violence in the United States continue to sound an alarm that is being echoed in countries around the world. Though the statistics vary from

Teen use of illegal drugs spans both genders and all socioeconomic and ethnic groups.

year to year and from community to community, they reveal a picture that cannot be dismissed by anyone concerned about the future of our children and youth.

Alcohol and Drugs

- About 10 million drinkers are younger than twenty-one years old. Of these, 4.4 million are binge drinkers (five or more drinks at once in a month), including 1.7 million heavy drinkers (five or more drinks at once at least five times in a month). [1]
- Forty-seven percent of boys from grades ten through twelve consider themselves "drinkers." The reasons they give for drinking range from peer and academic pressures to boredom and rebellion. [2]
- About 4.5 million twelve- to seventeen-year-olds are smokers. [3]
- The number of youths who have used illicit drugs in the last month doubled from 1992 to 1995. [4]
- The main risk factors for drug abuse are boredom, lack of parental support, feelings of failure, and social pressure. [5]

Sexuality

- The U.S. has more than double the teen pregnancy rate of any Western industrialized nation. [6]
- Every year, about 175,000 girls seventeen years old and younger have their first baby. [7]
- Adult men (men over the age of twenty) are responsible for two-thirds of all teen pregnancies. [8]
- Teens have the highest rates of sexually transmitted diseases of any age group, with one in every four teens getting an STD by age twenty-one. [9]
- Every day, between twenty-seven and fifty-four people under the age of twenty in the U.S. are infected by HIV. This is more than two youngsters every hour. [10]

Violence

- Seventy-four percent of junior high and high school students in this country say teenage violence and crime is a major problem. [11]
- Twenty-six percent of fourteen- to seventeen-year-old boys say they or their friends had been the victims of gang violence. [12]
- More than one in four high school students will be a victim of physical violence perpetrated by someone he or she dates. [13]
- There are as many youths in prison as there are residents in Rhode Island. [14]
- We spend $30,000 per year, per individual, to incarcerate young people. That's ten times what we spend on their education. [15]

The problems are grave, and they cut across income levels, race, religions, ethnic groups, and educational levels. Even teens who have always behaved well and achieved success can still make a bad choice or become the victim of someone else's bad choice. As parents, we must do all we can to help reduce the risks.

How Alcohol and Other Drugs Can Hurt Teenagers

Physical Effects

- Smoking cigarettes causes lung cancer and heart disease. Just because your teen is young doesn't mean he's not hurting himself by smoking.

- Using marijuana damages teens' ability to remember and their ability to learn.

- Most drugs are addictive either physically or psychologically. Your teen may not acknowledge that she is addicted, or she may not seem to be addicted, but her denial could be part of her addiction. Any teen smoking cigarettes or using drugs is at risk of mental addiction (believing she needs to keep using drugs to feel okay) and physical addiction.

- The more your teen drinks or uses drugs, the more tolerant he will think he is to these substances. As time goes on, he will need more and more drinks, drugs, snorts—whatever—to get the high he had when he first started using. Heavy users in particular also often combine drugs to get stronger results, which can be deadly.

- Alcohol and other drugs distort teens' perceptions, which can lead to dangerous behavior. For example, an intoxicated teen driving home from a party may think that he is driving as well as a professional race car driver, when in fact he isn't perceiving his speed or reactions accurately.

Psychological and Social Effects

- If your teen uses drugs to feel comfortable around others, he will not learn essential social skills. Instead, he will grow to need the drug or drink or cigarette on every date or at every party simply to be able to talk to others.

- Teens who drink or use drugs often lose interest in school. Their grades fall. Often they drop out of school.

- Teen users intentionally weaken their ties to family, friends, outside interests, values, and goals.

- Drug and alcohol use reduces inhibitions. This often leads to more dangerous drug use, more unprotected sexual activity, and more participation in reckless, violent situations (including becoming a victim).

- Drug and heavy alcohol use among teens leads to self-destructive thinking and behavior. Teens who use alcohol and drugs are more likely to consider, attempt, and succeed at suicide than teens who don't use.

41

Stages of Drug Use

Drug use frequently progresses in four stages:

① Experimentation

Nearly all teens will try alcohol or marijuana. This is not to say that all of them suffer from low self-esteem and discouragement. The majority are motivated by simple curiosity. They have seen alcohol used by the adults in their lives and have watched alcohol and drugs used in TV and movies for years (often, unfortunately, in an overly glamorized way). They wonder, "what's it like?" They see that "everyone tries it."

② Social Use

About three-fourths of the teens who enter the experimentation phase move on to stage two—social use. These teens will use alcohol and other drugs at parties and other social settings, often mimicking behavior they see around them.

③ Seeking

In this third phase, teens will actively seek out places where drugs can be found. It is usually in this phase that the addiction process begins.

④ Habitual Use

Teens who move into the habitual-use phase are no longer capable of making a free choice. The alcohol or other drug has become an addiction.

Fortunately, although a teen can go through all four stages in just a few months, the progression is not inevitable. Drug use can be stopped at any stage. However, the more involved young people are with drugs, the more difficult it is for them to stop. The best way to fight drug use, therefore, is to prevent it. Educating children about the harmful effects of drugs long before the teen years is ideal. If that isn't possible, however, there is still a lot that we can do.

Getting Help

If your relationship with your teen has deteriorated to the point that she is "out of control" (ignores your authority and does what she pleases) or if you suspect that she may be harming herself or in danger, you will want to get professional help. Start by calling your teen's school counselor, psychologist, or social worker, the local community mental health center, a private therapist specializing in adolescents, or your family physician. If problems persist, residential treatment in a hospital, therapeutic program, or other setting may be called for. Your first-level helper can assist you in finding a resource that fits your needs and budget. You can also refer to the list of hotline numbers in the appendix of this book.

Family Enrichment Activity: Getting to Know Your Teen Better

Ever notice that a good salesperson will always spend time developing a positive relationship with you before she tries to sell you anything? She knows that half the job of effectively influencing a person is first developing a positive relationship. Once the person has been "won over," the sale is much easier.

(Can you imagine a salesperson being autocratic and demanding a sale? "You'll buy this because I'm the salesperson and I said so!")

The same is true for parenting. The more you can enrich your relationship with your teen, the more influence he will allow you in his life. A healthy relationship will prevent many problems as well as make discipline much easier when you need to use it.

Taking the time to learn some of your teen's many characteristics can be enjoyable for both of you!

In each chapter we will present a Family Enrichment Activity for you to add to your parental tool chest. Use these and the other support skills in this book to strengthen your relationship. If your teen is frequently out of control, this may be a way to begin making positive contact. Be creative. And reach out.

Our first Family Enrichment Activity is designed to help you get to know your teen better through a casual interview about your teen's interests and activities. Asking about her interests says that you value her as a unique individual. To make the process of talking together as easy as possible, we've constructed some questions for you to use when you interview your teen. First, fill out the answers yourself. Then ask your teen for a time that you can conduct your "interview." After you've heard your teen's answers, you can share your responses and compare how close (or not so close!) you were.

Getting to Know Your Teen Better

Tips:

- Keep the activity on a positive note. Avoid judging your teen or making negative remarks about any of her answers.
- If you have more than one teen, conduct your interviews separately. This will make each child feel more special.
- Add some of your own questions, but don't get too heavy at this time (unless your teen initiates a weighty topic).

Parent's Questions:

1. Who is your teen's best friend?_____

_____

2. What does your teen like about him?_____

_____

3. What does he like about your teen?_____

_____

4. What is your teen good at?_____

_____

5. What does your teen worry about?_____

_____

6. What do you do that drives your teen crazy?_____

_____

7. How would your teen like to contribute to society as he grows older?_____

_____

_____

_____

_____

Teen's Questions:

1. Who is your best friend?_____

2. What do you like about him?_____
_____
_____
_____

3. What does your best friend like about you?_____
_____
_____
_____

4. What are you good at?_____
_____
_____
_____

5. What do you worry about?_____
_____
_____
_____

6. What do your parents do that drives you crazy?_____
_____
_____
_____

7. How would you like to contribute to society as you grow older?_____
_____
_____
_____

Chapter 1

Home Activities

If you haven't started practicing what you've learned from this chapter with your family, then now is the best time to put these ideas to work! Take the time to complete the following activities, then record your thoughts about these activities in the spaces indicated. You may feel a little unsure about your abilities to use these new skills. Like most new tasks, the more you practice them, the easier they'll become. Remember, the sooner you start changing your behavior toward your teen, the sooner your teen will start changing her behavior toward you!

1. Reread any section from this chapter that you would like to be reminded about.
2. Do the Family Enrichment Activity: Getting to Know Your Teen Better, on pages 45 and 46.
3. Give your teen some choices over the next few days, then complete the Choices Practice sheet on page 33.
4. Read on!

Courage and Self–Esteem

Chapter 2

Courage and Self-Esteem

Fifteen-year-old Josh had been having a very bad week. First, a "D" on his biology test. "Guess I should have studied," he thought to himself gloomily. To make matters worse, his younger sister, Jackie, came home with an "A" on her social studies test. The way his parents were crowing over her was enough to make him sick. He tried to cheer himself up by playing with his little brother Andrew. Andrew had always looked up to Josh. But this time Andrew started teasing Josh about his acne. Which really ticked him off. So naturally Josh poked Andrew, barely. The little baby ran crying to Mom and Dad, saying Josh hit him really hard. Of course Josh got blamed. For what? Just because he was bigger? Life was definitely not fair in this family.

Josh moodily strolled to the mirror to check himself out. Yeah, breaking out all over. What a loser. Well, at least he had a good body, he told himself as he flexed a muscle. Isn't that what girls were supposed to care about? Then his heart sank as he remembered the teasing from his best friend, Steve. "If you get out of tenth grade still a virgin, I'm gonna kick your butt." Steve had had sex for the first time in eighth grade. He had a lot of confidence around girls. Which of course I don't, thought Josh. He remembered the upcoming party on Saturday night. Maybe it could happen with Jennifer that night. This was their third date. Maybe if he could get her to down a couple of beers.

Courage: One from the Heart

Teens easily lose their courage. Even minor events can quickly turn feelings of courage into feelings of discouragement.

Fifteen years old doesn't sound very fun right now, does it? Although it may not seem like it, Josh lacks courage. In other words, he is very discouraged. Like most teens, he is struggling to balance the pressures of school, a social life, and his family with the rapid changes he is experiencing in his own intellectual, physical, and emotional development. His failures hit him particularly hard. He beats himself up with his own perceptions. He has lost heart.

In Chapter 1, I explained that the French word *coeur*, meaning heart, is the base of the English word *courage*. Just as the heart has long been considered the emotional center of a person, courage might be thought of as the core of a person's character.

Courage is intimately linked to fear. We experience them both throughout our lives at times of risk. Do I go ahead or turn back? What if I fail? Do I dare to take the chance? It is our courage that keeps us going when the easier path is to quit or give in to an unwise temptation. Because striving for most positive goals in life requires some risk, courage is essential. For a teen to become responsible, she has to risk the consequences of her choices. To cooperate, she has to risk that others may take advantage of her. Honesty, hard work, even love all require some risk.

Courage = the confidence to take a known risk for a known purpose.

This definition of courage is based on how well you understand your risk. If you don't know the consequences of a risk, then the act isn't courageous—it's foolish. You need to know the real reason for taking the risk too, because otherwise you're not being courageous—you're being reckless. For example, the teen who takes drugs for the thrill of it, thinking nothing bad will happen to her, is not being courageous. She doesn't know the real risks or real purpose. Instead she is being foolish and reckless. Contrast this with the teen who makes an "F" on a test but decides to study for hours to do better on the next one. He is showing a lot of courage.

Self–Esteem: One from the Mind

Where does this teen's courage come from? It comes from a belief in himself—a belief that he is a lovable, capable person who has a good chance to succeed. And when he doesn't succeed, he looks inward for a belief that he is much more than just his achievements —that there is something worthwhile and special about him just because he is himself. This belief—his self-esteem—helps motivate him to continue to work hard for good grades even after he has received a low one. It gives him the confidence to say "no" to his friends when they pressure him to use drugs.

When we have high self-esteem, we think we have a good chance to succeed, and we know that all is not lost if we don't. This confidence gives us the courage to take reasonable risks.

High Self-Esteem  **Courage.**

Unfortunately, the opposite is also true. When we think badly of ourselves—that we are unlovable and not capable—our self-esteem drops. This low self-esteem produces discouragement and fear.

Low Self-Esteem → leads to → Discouragement.

Teens with high self-esteem have the courage to take positive risks, while teens with low self-esteem don't bother taking risks, or they take unwise ones because they don't value themselves. For example:

A teen with high self-esteem:	A teen with low self-esteem:
• risks making mistakes in school by working hard and trying his best.	• develops an "I don't care" attitude and stops working or even drops out.
• does what she knows is right even if she loses her friends in the process.	• changes her values to conform to those of peers.
• cooperates with parents even when he doesn't always get his way.	• resents authority and rebels, either openly or passively, through failure and other means.
• finds positive ways, such as sports, to achieve such goals as independence and challenge.	• resorts to easier, negative behavior—including drugs, sexuality, and violence—to achieve the same goals.

The Think-Feel-Do Cycle

If you want to influence your teen, you first need to understand how her thoughts and feelings (including her self-esteem and courage) influence her behavior. Our thoughts and feelings often determine how we act. I have dubbed this sequence of thoughts, feelings, and actions the Think-Feel-Do Cycle.

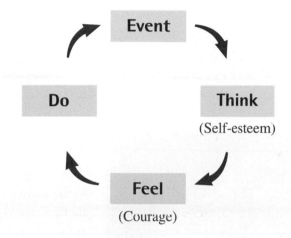

Start with an event. When something happens to your teen, she thinks about it, both consciously and unconsciously. These thoughts trigger an emotional response, a feeling about what happened. She then acts on that feeling. How she acts in turn influences another event to happen, which starts the Think-Feel-Do Cycle again.

Here's a simple example. Shelly is a quiet teen who one day approached someone new in the cafeteria and started a conversation. That's the event. The fact that she talked to a stranger led her to think she might be capable of socializing. That thought made her feel more confident in herself. With her new confidence, Shelly approached the same new student the next day to start a friendship. Thus a positive action begins a positive cycle, which then triggers additional positive events.

Let's see how the Think-Feel-Do Cycle reveals Josh's thought process.

Let's start with Josh's biology test. His thinking about this event may have included some of the following:

- Values: "Doing well in school is important."

- Beliefs: "I blew it. I knew I wasn't very smart. Jackie is the smart one in the family. I'm pretty pathetic."

These negative thoughts lowered his self-esteem and triggered negative feelings, such as discouragement, anger, sadness, worthlessness, and depression. These feelings led to more negative actions on Josh's part, as we will soon see.

Caught in a failure cycle, Josh reacts by displaying more negative behavior.

Of course, there is always more than one event going on at a time in a person's life. Josh is in the middle of lots of events that include his other school subjects, his family, his friends, and his social life. When more than one event goes sour at the same time, the resulting stress is multiplied. This happens to Josh as he thinks and feels about his acne, how he compares to his sister, and his lack of sexual experience.

Tolerating setbacks and disappointing events requires courage. When a teen's courage is low, he often looks for a quick way to reduce his pain. If he is talented in something, such as sports or music, he can focus on these as a positive way to help him feel better about himself. Unfortunately, teens often turn to negative behavior to get some temporary relief. Let's see how this plays out in Josh's case.

When Josh finally got out of bed Sunday morning, his head hurt and he had an empty feeling in the pit of his stomach. He cringed as the events of last night began to come back to him. How could he have been so stupid? Everything had been going great with Jennifer. Then he had started drinking. Well, so what, he thought as he walked to the mirror to examine his bleary eyes. It was a party, wasn't it? Josh sat back down on the edge of the bed and tried to remember what happened next. Oh yeah. He groaned. Steve had handed him the keys to his car and a condom. Why hadn't Josh just laughed and walked away?

He remembered that he and Jennifer were in the car outside the party, listening to music. He had gotten her to drink some beer. They had kissed. So far, so good. Then Josh had pulled out the condom. Jennifer seemed shocked. That wasn't part of the plan. Josh was a little fuzzy about what happened next. Did he actually grab her and try to force himself on her? Oh man, yes he did. She had pushed him away and beer had spilled all over the car. Josh seemed to remember her getting out of the car and calling him something—a stupid jerk. As he remembered the scene, Josh put his head in his hands. He fell back on the bed. Just let me curl up and die, he thought.

The Failure Cycle

When a teen reacts to events in his life with low self-esteem and a faulty belief system, the discouragement and negative behavior that follow usually produce more negative events. In Josh's case, these events might include getting dumped by Jennifer, increasing alcohol abuse, and more failed tests. In addition, teen misbehavior often provokes harsh criticism and punishment from autocratic adults. This triggers more faulty thinking and lower self-esteem, more discouragement, and more negative behavior and failure.

FAILURE CYCLE

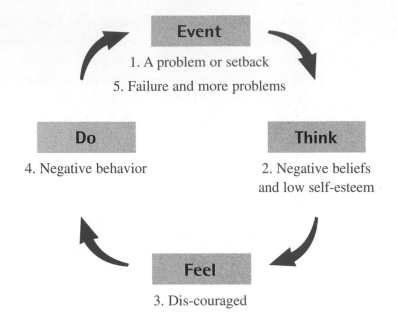

Event

1. A problem or setback

5. Failure and more problems

Do

4. Negative behavior

Think

2. Negative beliefs
and low self-esteem

Feel

3. Dis-couraged

The Success Cycle

A teen with higher self-esteem than Josh's and more positive beliefs about himself might have responded much differently to the failed biology test. He may have thought, "Face it. I blew it. I'll have to study big time for the next one to make up for it." Such thinking may have produced some feelings of remorse for having done poorly on the test, but not discouragement. In fact, a teen with high self-esteem and a good set of beliefs can take failure and turn it into a positive experience, one in which he learns from his mistakes. His positive behavior usually produces additional successful events, including positive feedback from adults. These successes strengthen self-esteem and courage, produce more effort and positive behavior, and thus more success. The saying "nothing succeeds like success" describes the success cycle.

High self-esteem gives Jennifer the courage to stand up for herself and resist pressure from Josh.

Jennifer is a good example of a teen in a success cycle. Her high self-esteem and mature attitude about sexuality gave her the courage to resist Josh's advances. She stood up for herself and took positive action to solve the problem by leaving. She will feel good when she thinks later about how she handled herself. Her self-esteem will strengthen, and she'll feel encouraged to stand up for herself the next time she is threatened.

SUCCESS CYCLE

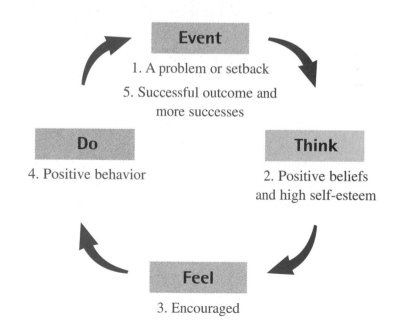

Event

1. A problem or setback

5. Successful outcome and more successes

Do

4. Positive behavior

Think

2. Positive beliefs and high self-esteem

Feel

3. Encouraged

Self–Esteem or Self–Hype?

Self-esteem has gotten a bad reputation recently because the term has been loosely invoked as a supposed fix to solve all types of problems. Even the TV show *Saturday Night Live* has pointed out the nonsense of such approaches in its parody featuring "Stuart Smalley," who tries to build his self-esteem by looking in the mirror and telling himself what a good person he is and that "people like me." Although it may be possible to fool the conscious mind temporarily with such hype, it is at the unconscious level where true self-esteem resides. Having a deep-seated sense that you are a worthwhile person derives from a strong core of character and values and the knowledge that your behavior is usually in line with those values. People with "event driven self-esteem" think: "when I do well, I feel worthwhile, but when I strike out, I feel worthless." With a solid sense of self-esteem, your highs and lows don't depend on the events in your life. A person with real self-esteem will know that she is worthwhile regardless of individual successes or failures.

Most teens are usually on a self-esteem roller coaster. They go up and down like the Scream Machine at the amusement park. When Josh flexed his muscles in the mirror, he was hyping himself into feeling a temporary self-esteem boost. If he had gotten Jennifer to have sex, he may have ridden the roller coaster back to the top for a brief while. But such valueless successes do not have a lasting effect. In fact, they often lower self-esteem in the long run.

Parents as Encouragers

When your teen is discouraged, you will want to help her break out of her failure cycle. When she's encouraged, you'll want to help her continue to thrive in her success cycle. To do both requires a skillful blend of **encouragement** and **discipline**. We'll cover discipline in the next chapter. For now, let's look at developing our encouragement skills.

There are many ways to encourage your children, and they all begin with the same first step: recognizing and avoiding ways that you inadvertently discourage them. (To en-courage actually means "to give courage"; to dis-courage means "to remove courage.")

Four Ways We Sometimes Discourage

It may not always seem like it, but parents are very important people in their teens' lives. What they say and do can have an enormous effect on their teens. Try putting yourself in a teen's shoes as you read about four of the most common ways parents discourage their teens. Then look for ways to catch yourself before you make these mistakes with your own children.

You may think you're helping your teen by focusing on how she can do better, but the result is often discouragement and more failure from your teen.

1. Focusing on mistakes and weaknesses

If someone important to you spends more time pointing out your faults than your strengths, you may come to believe there is much more wrong with you than right. If that important person yells or sounds disgusted with you, it hurts even more. If he calls you names and attacks your character, you may begin to believe you are as bad as he says.

Improvement begins to seem impossible. This is how a teen feels when his parent constantly points out the mistakes he makes.

Example:

"You are so lazy! I don't know why I even bother!"

"If you want to get anywhere, you're going to have to stop being so shy."

"I just can't see any reason for this C in geometry." (said while ignoring the A's and B's in other subjects)

2. Expecting the worst or too little

If you don't believe in your teen's abilities, your teen probably won't believe in them either. Parents don't always express these low expectations overtly, but teens get the message loud and clear.

If you expect the worst from your teen, he will probably do just what you fear.

"I knew you'd start cutting school like those losers you hang out with. Next, you'll be dropping out."

"You'd better stay out of trouble while I'm gone."

"Girls have a harder time in math than boys, so a C is pretty good."

3. Expecting too much

On the other hand, if you expect more from your child than she is able to give, she may gradually stop trying. No matter what she accomplishes, she will never satisfy you. Or so it seems to her. She may decide to stop trying and turn to excelling in negative ways, such as drug abuse, unhealthy sexual activity, or violence.

Some teens become perfectionists in a futile attempt to please their parents. Life becomes one big worry. Sadly, many young people seem to have it all together but actually have very fragile self-esteem. Some teenage girls take their perfection to a harmful extreme by losing all the weight they can and becoming anorexic. Some boys waiting to develop the "perfect" body turn to steroids to help them develop their muscles. In extreme cases, parents raise the level of expectation so high that their children conclude they are worthless and give up.

Example:

"Don't get conceited; you still have a lot of room for improvement."

"I'll bet if you lost five pounds, you'd look really good in that dress."

"You're already great in track. Why aren't you on the varsity soccer team?"

4. Overprotecting and pampering

If you are constantly telling your teen how dangerous the world is and preventing him from taking even reasonable risks, he may begin to believe that he can't handle things for himself. He may become extremely dependent on you and expect you to take over all his decisions. Alternatively, he may rebel and take reckless risks just to show that you can't run his life.

Many parents act more like personal servants than parents, providing wake-up service, maid service, taxi service without notice, short-order cooking, and any other buffers needed to protect their children from the realities of life. Not surprisingly, their children form unrealistic ideas about how the world works. When these teens grow up they are often unmotivated to work hard or do things for themselves. They expect things to be easy. When they aren't, they'll become frustrated and angry.

Example:

"If you're not ready to take that science test, why don't you let me write you a sick note so you can study some more?"

"Well, I really need to get this report done, but if it means that much to you, I'll drive you to the mall."

"I'm going to sit right here and help you with your homework like I always do."

Turning Discouragement into Encouragement

Fortunately, each of the four ways we often discourage teens can be turned around and become ways to encourage them:

Turn Discouragers　　　　　**Into Encouragers**

don't:　　　　　　　　　　　**do:**

1. Focus on mistakes and weaknesses

2. Expect the worst or too little

3. Expect too much

4. Overprotect and pamper

1. Build on strengths

2. Show confidence

3. Value the teen as is

4. Stimulate independence

These methods of encouraging are effective not only with our teens, but also with co-workers, spouses, and other adults. After all, who doesn't need some self-esteem and courage reinforcement sometimes? Let's look at them more closely.

(1.) Build on Strengths

If you want a teen to do better in general, find something you like about her. When we focus on a teen's strengths rather than her weaknesses, she feels encouraged to build more strengths.

"I really like your enthusiasm, the way you jump in with both feet."

"You have a great sense of humor."

"I have to tell you, even though we argue a lot, I really admire how you stand up for yourself. That will be valuable when others try to get you to do something you don't want to do."

Building on a teen's strengths also helps her improve a specific skill, value, or character trait. Whether you are helping a teen do better with a school subject or to be more respectful, keep in mind the following three steps.

1. Acknowledge what they do well.

Parents often make the mistake of waiting until their child can do something 100 percent before saying something encouraging. But a little encouragement along the way can make the difference between a teen giving up and struggling to succeed. Notice what your teen already does well and comment on this when you see it. Your encouragement will help give him the confidence and motivation to take the next step. This "catch 'em doing well" approach takes some practice, but it is key to building self-esteem and courage.

Example:

"Thank you for letting me know how you felt without yelling."

"I really like the way you described the old man's hands in your theme."

"Your bookshelves look very neat and well organized. It looks like you know where to find things."

"It was a pleasure having you with us at dinner. Not only were you very polite, but I thought you made a lot of good comments during the conversation."

"Thanks for getting in on time. I appreciate it."

"I appreciate your keeping it quiet while I took a nap. That was considerate."

2. Encourage the teen to take the next step.

Moving in a step-by-step process toward a goal is not easy. There are times when our courage or energy fails or when we just don't progress. During such times, it is easy to become disheartened and give up. This is when a word of encouragement from a parent or other significant person can help motivate teens to keep trying.

Example:

"Learning to do geometry can be frustrating, and I know you feel like giving up. But if you'll just stick with it, I know you can get it. Look how far you've come already!"

"The bookshelves look great. I'll help you with the closet next week."

"Come on! One more chin-up. You can do it!"

"You are sounding so good playing the piano. This piece is hard, but every day it seems to be getting a little easier for you!"

3. Concentrate on improvement, not the end result.

Any movement in a desired direction is worth acknowledging. Of course there will be times when your teen backslides to a previous level. When this happens, you can encourage by reminding her that progress is usually an up-and-down process, not a straight line.

Example:

"I know you feel bad striking out three times in the game. But you've been doing really well lately. With a little practice I know you can straighten your swing out again."

"Yesterday when you were upset about my not being able to take you and Kevin to the movies, you stayed respectful. Thanks."

2. Show Confidence

Teens develop self-esteem and courage by learning how to handle problems and develop skills. But to do this, they need self-esteem and courage. You can cut into this "chicken and egg" situation by giving responsibility, asking your teen's opinion or advice, and avoiding unnecessary rescues.

By asking your teen what he thinks, you let him know that you value his opinion and trust him with the responsibility of making decisions.

Give responsibility.

Giving your teen responsibility is a nonverbal way of showing confidence. It says, "I know you can do this." Of course, be careful to give responsibilities that are in line with the teen's age and level of ability, or you are setting him up for failure.

Example:

"It would be a big help if you would take over cooking dinner one night a week."

"Would you be willing to take responsibility for the garage sale? I'll help if you need it, but I've got so much to do this week, and I know you'd do a good job."

"I'll agree to your going to the party if you'll agree that if there's any alcohol or other drugs there, you will call us to pick you up immediately."

Ask your teen's opinion or advice.

The teen years are filled with rapid intellectual growth. You can help encourage this development, as well as the self-esteem and courage that can go with it, by asking your teen's opinion or advice. You can even ask her to teach you something.

Example:

"You seem to be good at using the Internet. Would you show me how to get some information about this topic?"

"Something came up at work today, and I wanted to know what you thought about it."

"Now that you'll be dating soon, we'd like your help in setting some guidelines so that we can all feel comfortable with the situation."

A word of caution: Be careful to avoid turning your teen into a confidante or best friend. Sharing intimate personal problems can sometimes feel good, especially for a single parent, but it can be an unfair burden on your teen. Look for a close friend or a counselor for this type of adult sharing.

Avoid unnecessary rescues.

Some problems require parental involvement. But sometimes your children can solve problems on their own. When you refuse to step in and take over when your teen becomes frustrated or discouraged, you're showing confidence in her abilities. You're offering support and encouragement without robbing her of the self-esteem that comes from struggle and success.

Example:

"Keep trying. You can do it!"

"I know this is hard for you. Can you think of anything that would help you work it out?"

3. Value Your Teen as Is

The most valuable gift you can give your teen is unconditional love.

As we've stated earlier, your teen's self-esteem does not come from his achievements alone. What's more important to him is to be accepted by significant people in his life. In fact, this is what most people want most —to be accepted for who they really are, not just for what they've accomplished.

Teens who feel accepted by their parents have a sturdy foundation of self-esteem on which they can base a happy, healthy life. Without this foundation, even the richest, most successful person often leads a miserable life, wondering why her successes aren't satisfying.

Our goal, then, is to show our teens that win or lose, pass or fail, in trouble or out of trouble, we are still their parents, and **we are glad of it**. Everyone needs this unconditional love from someone. This is why parenting programs that advocate kicking a rebellious teen out of the house are off the mark. No one should ever communicate to his teen that she is no longer part of the family. Parents should say just the opposite: "No matter what it takes—counseling, hospitalization, a therapy program—we're going to find a way for you to be a part of this family. We love you, and we're going to get you the help you need."

Fortunately, most families don't reach this stage. But all parents need to look at the subtle messages they give their teens and focus on ways to value them just because they are your children. Here are some ideas.

Separate the deed from the doer.

Teens feel good when they learn that they are much more than just the sum of their behavior—that they are loved and valued for themselves. We can help them realize their intrinsic worth by separating who they are from what they do.

When your teen misbehaves, focus your attention on the behavior, not the teen.

Example:

This: "I don't like you talking to me that way. It's rude."
Not this: "You are so rude."

This: "You failed the test because you didn't study enough, not because you're dumb."
Not this: "If you weren't so lazy, you'd have passed this test."

Even when encouraging your teen's positive behavior, you still need to focus your attention on the behavior, not the teen. Why? Because a teen's subconscious reasons like this: "If I'm good when I do good, then I must be bad when I do bad." Once a teen concludes he is somehow bad, he gives up. You want your child to learn that he is always a good person, but that he sometimes chooses bad behavior. His choices are correctable.

This: "That was really considerate of you to take your brother with you."
Not this: "You are such a considerate person."

This: "I really appreciate the way you help out around here."
Not this: "You are such a helpful young man."

We can also help our teens learn to separate actions from self-worth by gently correcting them when they get down on themselves.

Example:

"Missing two foul shots doesn't make a person a loser. It can happen to the best players, too."

"You're not stupid. You made a mistake. If you were stupid you'd make the same mistake over and over again. I think you've learned something and will make a different choice next time."

Appreciate your teen's uniqueness.

Although we live in a society of equals, that doesn't mean we are all the same. It is important for your teen to know that she is unique, special, and one-of-a-kind, with her own dreams and talents. You can appreciate your teen's uniqueness by showing an interest in her activities. Most of all, you can say and do things that show your teen you love her for her own unique self, and for no other reason.

"When I see you from a distance I can tell it's you by your walk."

"This room really is you! I could never have decorated it for you."

"What do you dream about doing someday?"

"You are the only you in the whole world. I'm so glad that you are my daughter!"

"I love you."

(4.) Stimulate Independence

Teens work hard to break away from their parents and become independent adults. The more they succeed, the higher their self-esteem and courage will rise. Give your teen some independence and freedom—it will also reduce how much the two of you fight. Keeping a teen overly dependent upon a parent usually backfires. As psychologist Hiam Ginott once wrote, "Dependence breeds hostility." The last thing we want is to keep our teens overly dependent on us. (Unless, of course, you want to someday have a hostile thirty-year-old living with you.)

Example:

"I think going to camp for four weeks is a great idea. Let's talk about how you can help pay for it."

"I'm okay with you taking a part-time job as long as it's no more than twenty hours a week and doesn't affect you schoolwork."

"Consider this fair warning: From now on, when you want me to drive you somewhere, you need to let me know in advance and not expect me to drop what I'm doing to take you."

"Running this house is the responsibility of all of us. I'd like us to have a family meeting to discuss which chores each of us will be doing."

Stimulate Independence

Think of things you are doing for your teen that she could be doing herself (for example, making her bed, picking up her clothes, and paying for personal items). Make a list below.

1. _____
2. _____
3. _____
4. _____
5. _____

Now turn these items over to your teen. Be sure to do it in a polite, encouraging way so your teen feels like she's gaining some independence instead of being punished.

Example:

"From now on, Dennis, I want to hand over the responsibility of picking up your clothes to you. I know you can handle it."

Afterwards, write your feelings below.

What did you like about what happened?_____

_____

_____

_____

What can you do to improve things next time?_____

_____

_____

Allow your teen to take reasonable risks.

Give your teen freedom within limits you feel are reasonable.

Remember that courage is about having the confidence to take reasonable risks. Talk with other adults, including parents and educators, to get a feel for what others think are reasonable limits and freedoms for teens of different ages. Then talk with your teen about guidelines and expectations for different situations (more on these "prevention talks" in Chapter 3). The key is to allow your teen more and more independence from you while staying aware of how she handles each new step. If she does not handle the independence well, you can return to tighter limits next time. If she handles the independence responsibly, she has earned the right to have more.

Example:

"You may go to the concert as long as you follow the guidelines we've discussed."

"The choice to play football is yours, but I'd like to talk with you about other sports that have less risk for a major injury."

"Going to camp is a great way to develop your independence. So is getting a part-time job to help pay for it."

Help your teen develop a sense of independence.

The truth is that life in a democratic society is neither dependent

73

nor independent. It is interdependent. One of the things this means for teens is that along with their emerging independence comes a desire to belong to new groups of friends. The ability to work with others becomes important around this time too. We can help encourage the give and take necessary for being a friend and working with others cooperatively.

Example:

"You are an important part of this family, and we'd like your input at family council meetings." (Family meetings are presented in Chapter 6.)

"Would you like to help change the oil in the car?"

"Would you like me to help the two of you work out a fair plan for sharing the telephone?"

Sharing a task, like changing the oil, does so much more than simply getting the job done!

Encouragement Profile

Everyone has abilities, talents, and positive qualities. Think about these qualities in your teen and yourself and write some below, filling in names as you go.

_____ does well at _____

_____.

I do well at _____

_____.

_____ helps me _____

_____.

I help _____ with _____

_____.

_____ is learning _____

_____.

I am learning _____

_____.

A strength _____ has is _____

_____.

One of my strengths is _____

_____.

_____ can _____.

I can _____

_____.

_____ learned how to _____

_____.

What I like best about _____ is _____

_____.

What I like best about myself is_____

_____.

Encouragement Chart

Practice using encouraging statements with your teen right away. To help you stay aware of your own efforts to be more encouraging, fill out the chart below each time you encourage your teen. It's important!

Teen's Name	Day	Encouraging Statement
_____	____	_____
_____	____	_____
_____	____	_____
_____	____	_____
_____	____	_____
_____	____	_____
_____	____	_____
_____	____	_____
_____	____	_____
_____	____	_____
_____	____	_____
_____	____	_____
_____	____	_____
_____	____	_____
_____	____	_____
_____	____	_____
_____	____	_____
_____	____	_____
_____	____	_____
_____	____	_____
_____	____	_____

Self-Esteem and Teenage Girls

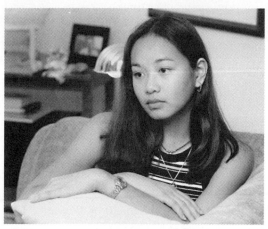

Girls' self-esteem in our society is often harder hit during adolescence than boys' self-esteem.

A growing body of evidence suggests that many girls in this country experience a loss of self-esteem when they hit adolescence. Girls who at ten were active, confident, and enthusiastic about learning change drastically in the early teen years, becoming less curious, less concerned about their long-term goals, and more worried about how they look and what others think about them. This shift happens to boys, too, but studies show that in boys it isn't as severe or prolonged. Why does this happen to our daughters?

Consider the female image presented in our media. Everywhere girls look—on billboards, in magazines, on TV—they see women whose primary function is to be beautiful and sexy. Pictures of women are often altered to create unrealistic perfection: Skin tone, eye and hair color, even the length of women's legs are often changed in print advertising. Supermodels often lead drastic lifestyles to support their body image, including drug use and operations to remove ribs. At a time when adolescent girls are naturally putting on fat and are going through other hormonal changes, they are bombarded with images of women too thin to menstruate. Most adults realize that these are not realistic images of women, but many teen girls don't know that. Little wonder that so many teenage girls become bulimic or anorexic in an attempt to stay thin.

Perhaps more damaging than these artificial images are the messages girls continue to receive about their role in society. One of my colleagues recently overheard a mother telling her teenage daughter not to worry about going to college, but to find a rich man to marry instead. This traditional message—that a woman's role is to support a man emotionally while he takes care of her financially—is still alive and well. A little girl who grew up dreaming of being an astronaut now spends her time as a teen trying to get and keep the attention of boys instead of learning physics. Even though you may not say something as obvious as the above statement to your daughter, she's still getting the message from other sources, and perhaps more subtly from you.

Help Your Teen Break from the Gender Stereotype.

What can you do to help counteract some of the negative messages society heaps on girls and boys about what it means to be women and men? Here are some ideas:

- Value your teenage girl's skills, especially academic abilities.
- Encourage her to be assertive about what she wants and needs, not just to support others.
- Encourage her to play one or more sports.
- Help her set long-term goals about what will make her happy, which may not include marriage and a family.
- Discuss with her what she needs to reach these goals.
- Expect as much from your daughter as your son.
- Teach your son to respect girls as equals, not as sexual objects.
- Help your son and/or your daughter see how the media overemphasizes looks and paints an unrealistic picture of thinness.
- Encourage your son to participate in the arts and to express himself through drawing, writing, and similar pursuits.
- Teach teens of both sexes to notice and name their feelings, and treat these feelings as important information for understanding themselves and others.
- Provide your son with information about career options that are traditionally female, such as nursing, parenting or child care, social work, and elementary education.

- Provide your daughter with information about career options that are traditionally male, such as science, finance, professional cooking, piloting, and business management.
- Help your son be comfortable with his body image and physical development.
- Help your son understand that all boys don't have sex before they leave high school.

Drugs, Sexuality, and Violence: Why Teens Get Involved

For many teens, peer pressure can be very strong, often stronger than a parent's influence.

Many teens are misinformed about the true risks of drug use, unsafe sex, and criminal involvement. But many others are well aware of what can happen from a single overdose, a drunk driving accident, an HIV infection, or a serious fight. Why, then, do they get involved? Teens mistakenly believe they can get around the dangers and escape unharmed. "It won't happen to me" is an almost universal thought among teens. They feel they are invincible. Also, let's face it, experimenting with drugs and sex can be enjoyable and exciting. Media images reinforce the glamour.

Drugs, Sexuality, and Violence:
The Think–Feel–Do Cycle

The more troubled a teenager is, the more vulnerable he is to the lure of drugs, sex, and violence. A teen with low self-esteem can lose himself in the pleasure or excitement of drugs, sexuality, or violence and so escape the pain and insecurity of self-doubt.

Let's consider the Think-Feel-Do Cycle again. Imagine the typical "failure cycle" of a teen boy who is shy around girls and hasn't the confidence or skills to approach them. He's at a party and is offered a beer.

Read the cycle clockwise, one number at a time.

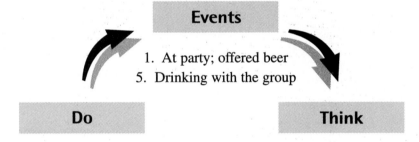

Events

1. At party; offered beer
5. Drinking with the group

Do

4. He drinks a beer.
8. He's now laughing and having fun with guys and girls . . . and having another beer.

Think

2. "Yeah, everyone else is drinking."
6. "This is cool. Maybe I'll have another."

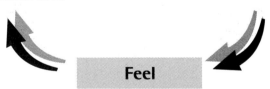

Feel

3. Relieved to be fitting in
7. A little high from the beer and less self-conscious around girls

We've all heard of alcohol giving a person "courage." This allows the drinker a short-cut to developing real skills (such as social skills in this case) and real courage. But to maintain the illusion, the drinker has to keep getting high on alcohol or other drugs. This is where the addiction process starts. As the teen becomes addicted, crucial opportunities to develop social and emotional skills are lost.

The same thing can happen with sex. The pleasure and thrill of sex can be so stimulating that many teenagers use sex to temporarily forget their problems. Often, sex is used as a confidence-booster.

The encouragement skills presented in this chapter are critical to the prevention of alcohol and drug abuse, unhealthy sexual activity, and violence. The more you help your teen build a strong sense of self-esteem and courage, the less tempting these dangerous activities become.

Ten Prevention Strategies for Parents

Strategy #1. Be a positive role model and teacher of values.

Your teen is just now learning how to act like an adult. Because adult decisions and choices are new to him, he needs values and beliefs that he can base his actions on when he's not sure what to do. As the most important person in your teen's life, you can help him form these values by talking with him about issues and setting a good example yourself.

Imagine that you and your teen are watching a movie together when one of the characters lights up a cigarette. This is a great opportunity to influence your teen. You could say, "How can they show cigarette smoking looking so cool when it's killing this guy? It wouldn't look cool if they flashed ahead twenty years to when he's dying in pain from cancer." Without directly confronting your teen, you have given him something to think about. You can also have a family talk later in which you can present other evidence about the harmful effects of tobacco. (We'll discuss "family talks" in Chapter 6.)

What you do shows your teen your values much stronger than what you say.

Of course your words would ring hollow if two minutes later you lit up a cigarette yourself. *What you do shows your teen your values much stronger than what you say.* You are your teen's role model. What do you model for your teen through your behavior? Do you "walk your talk"? As someone once said: "Values aren't taught; they're caught." What we teach our teens about the use of tobacco, alcohol, and other drugs is as much about our own behavior as is it about what we say we value.

Example:

If a parent uses illegal substances, a teen learns that it's not important to abide by the law. If the parent can sneak, the teen concludes that she can sneak too.

If a father treats women as sexual objects, making crude remarks and sexist comments, the teen concludes that women are not worthy of respect.

If a parent flies off the handle in rage when things do not go her way, the teen learns to use intimidation to bully people into giving in.

If a parent gets drunk, the teen believes that it's okay to use alcohol without limits.

On the other hand:

If a parent follows the law and expresses disapproval of a character who breaks the law in a television show or movie, the teen learns that laws (and rules) are to be obeyed.

If a father treats women respectfully, avoiding crude remarks and expressing disapproval when other men make such remarks, the teen learns that men should treat women with respect.

If a parent is patient and uses peaceful methods to resolve conflicts, the teen learns to manage anger effectively and solve problems without violence.

If a parent drinks in moderation and discusses why adults can but teens can't, the teen learns how to be a responsible drinker. Of course, if parents choose to refrain from all drinking, they will model abstinence to their children.

You are the best role model for your teen.

If a parent's behavior is in line with what the parent says she values, the teen learns that the parent has integrity and will value her opinions and advice because the teen knows they are backed up by the parent's actions.

Parent Role-Model Questionaire for Chemical Use

There are no right or wrong answers to the following questions. They are designed to help you be aware of your use of chemicals and, as you reflect on your responses, what messages you may be sending your children as a role model.

1. Do you drink alcohol? How many drinks do you have a week?_____

2. Do you use alcohol or other drugs to comfort yourself when you're depressed?_____

3. Have your children ever seen you drunk?_____

4. Is there a difference between a social drinker and an abusive drinker? If yes, what is it?____
_____
_____

5. Do you unconsciously go to social functions where there is a lot of drinking and avoid ones where there is little or no drinking?_____

6. When you have friends over, do you immediately offer them an alcoholic drink?_____

7. In your home, do people joke about getting drunk and doing crazy things? ("Man, Jack got so drunk last night he . . .")._____

8. Do your children ever hear you arguing with your spouse about one or the other having had too much to drink?_____

9. Do you smoke cigarettes? How many a day?_____

10. Have you ever warned your children about smoking while you were smoking? How about drinking?_____

11. Do you routinely take a sleeping pill to fall asleep? Do you routinely use something to stay awake (amphetamines, coffee, cola)?_____
_____

12. When you are nervous or upset, is your immediate response to "take something" to get rid of the feeling?_____
_____

13. When you begin a diet, is your first thought to buy diet pills?_____

14. Do you drive when under the influence of alcohol or other mood-altering drugs?_____

15. Do you ride with drivers who are under the influence?_____

Family Enrichment Activity: Letter of Encouragement

I discovered a powerful method of encouragement many years ago as a young Sunday school teacher. At the end of the school year I decided to write each of my students a letter about the progress they had made during the year. As I wrote the letters, I found myself focusing only on the students' strengths and what I liked about them. These "letters of encouragement," as we now call them, were politely received as the students left for summer vacation.

A letter for your teen is more than just words on a page— it shows your teen how much you care about her!

I didn't think much more about these letters until four years later. I was at a reception when a woman approached me and introduced herself as the mother of one of my students from that Sunday school class. "That letter you wrote Alice," she said, "meant so much to her. You know, she still has it pinned to her bulletin board."

What I learned from that experience is that "putting it in writing" carries extra weight in our society, and that this is as true with encouragement as it is anything else. In addition, when you write a letter of encouragement, your teen can refer to it in the future and rekindle the warm feelings it generated, just as Alice did.

This chapter's family enrichment activity is to write each of your teens a letter of encouragement. Keep in mind these guidelines as you do:

- Write about improvement, not necessarily an accomplishment, in a particular area.
- Write only truthful comments. Don't say your teen has improved when he hasn't.
- Be specific about what the improvements are.
- Say how your child's behavior has been helpful to others.

Let's look at two examples. The first is for a young teen already in a success cycle:

Dear Megan,

Every day I am amazed at how many positive ways you are growing. You show you are responsible in keeping up with your schoolwork, and your grades reflect that effort. More important, you are learning so much about the world and how it works. I've even learned some myself from our conversations about what you are studying!

I also admire how much you are improving in softball. Your throwing is so much stronger than it was just last year, and you are making contact with the ball almost every time at bat now. I really enjoy coming to your games and can't believe that they can be so exciting. But why not? Your team has one of my favorite all-time athletes: YOU!

One other thing that I've noticed is how patient you are with your younger brother. When I saw you helping him with his reading the other day, I thought how lucky he was to have you for a big sister. Then I thought how lucky we are all to have you in our family.

Oh, one more thing: I really, really love you.

Dad

The next example is for an older teen who is working his way out of a failure cycle:

Dear Steve,

I just wanted to let you know that I appreciate the effort you've been making at controlling your temper. You haven't blown up in over two weeks. In fact you've had some really good ideas for solving problems around here. For example, your suggestion that you could take your sister to her party and pick her up if you could use the car for some errands in between worked out for everyone.

I also wanted to tell you how much I admire the effort you are putting into your schoolwork lately. You've really kept to the study time we set up, and it's starting to pay off. It takes a lot of courage to try your best at something that isn't easy or fun, and I know you'd rather spend the time with your friends. That's what makes your hard work so special.

Anyway, I just wanted you to know that I appreciate the effort. If I can do anything to help, let me know.

Love,

Mom

Chapter 2 | *Home Activities*

If you haven't started practicing what you've learned from this chapter with your family, take the time to put these ideas to work now. Complete the following activities, then record your thoughts about these activities in the spaces indicated.

1. Re-read any parts of this chapter for which you may need refreshing.
2. Write a Letter of Encouragement to your teen.
3. Think about how you may be subtly discouraging your teen and try to avoid doing so.
4. Complete the Parent Role-Model Questionnaire on page 84.
5. Complete the Encouragement chart on page 76 as you find ways to encourage your teen.

Courage and Fear

part one: **The Early Years**

Courage first met fear
When I was still a child;
Courage gazed with cool, clear eyes;
Fear was something wild.

Courage urged "Let's go ahead";
Fear said "Let's turn back."
Courage spoke of what we had,
Fear of what we lacked.

Courage took me by the hand
And warmed my frozen bone;
Yet Fear the while tugged at my legs
And whispered "We're alone."

Many have been the obstacles
Since first I had to choose,
And sometimes when Courage led me on
I've come up with a bruise.

And many have been the challenges
Since Fear and Courage met,
And yet those times I've followed Fear,
Too often tagged along Regret.

part two: *The Teen Years*

Courage met Fear once again
When I became a teen.
One spoke softly to my heart.
One whispered, low and mean.

Courage said, "Give me your best."
Fear shrugged, "Why? What for?"
Courage said, "You can, you will."
Fear said, "What a bore."

Courage looked me in the eye
And never let me quit
Even when the times were tough
And the lessons hurt a bit.

Fear was always waiting
With new ways to be cool:
Sex and drugs; booze, a smoke
And raising hell at school.

And if I hesitated
'Cause the Piper would be paid,
He'd scowl disgustedly and say,
"What's the matter? You afraid?"

I've learned a bit of wisdom
Since my childhood long ago.
I know what's right and wrong
When to stand up and say "No."

Because Courage doesn't mean
You never feel the fear.
It means you do what must be done
On the road that's right and clear.

It means you sometimes take a chance
Though often you may fail.
And if you do, you get back up
And work 'til you prevail.

Nor does Courage ever mean
Taking stupid dares and risks.
Trust your conscience and remember
That Courage sometimes means: resist.

Others may deride you
And you may often stand alone,
But Courage means you stand up proud
And pull the sword from the stone.

And so the battle rages
Since the day the two foes met,
And every time I let Fear win,
I pay with my regret.

But when I follow Courage
With a spirit brave and true,
I hear these words upon the wind:
There's nothing you can't do.

Michael H. Popkin

Teen Behavior and Problem Solving

Chapter 3

Behavior Is Goal Driven

When your teen misbehaves, it's not simply to defy you. He's probably achieving an underlying goal.

An almost universal complaint that parents of teens voice to me is that they don't understand what motivates their teens. "Why did she do *that*?" they ask. Or, even more frequently, "Why won't he just do (such and such)?" Parents want to know what their teens really care about and why they do what they do. When discussing motivation, it is important to understand that past events *do not directly cause our behavior*. What happened in the past may influence our thinking, but we are free to choose our future behavior based on our experience, values, and goals. To understand why people, including teenagers, behave the way they do, we should always ask ourselves, "What are their goals?"

Because many of our important goals influence our behavior at an unconscious level, it is often difficult to know what motivates someone. For example, fourteen-year-old Jason insists on getting a tattoo because all the other guys in his group are doing it. His parents are furious and absolutely forbid it. Jason does it anyway.

Why has Jason refused to comply with his parents' orders? What is his purpose, or goal? To help us answer these questions, let's talk a little about the psychology of teenagers' behavior. Experts have identified five basic goals that motivate young people to behave in certain ways.

Five Goals of Teen Behavior

Goal 1: Contact/Belonging

The basic need of every human being is to belong. This need begins as tiny babies, when we cannot survive without other people. As we grow, we continue to need other people. Although some of us live solitary lives, the vast majority of us live in groups. Our need is not just to belong, but also to make contact—physical and emotional—with other human beings.

As a baby, your child needed to be held—it was actually critical to his survival. Later, contact with you helped him develop a sense of belonging to the family, which gave him the self-esteem and courage he needed to interact with people outside the family. Up to that point, your child's need to belong was centered on you.

Your teen knows, at least unconsciously, that a successful future depends on moving out of the nest and belonging to other groups besides his family.

During the teen years, though, this changes. Friends suddenly become more important than family. This is tough for many parents to accept. Why would my teen rather just "hang out" with the guys than go with us to the park? *Because he knows, at least unconsciously, that a successful future depends on moving out of the nest and belonging to other groups besides his family.* Certainly family activities have a place in this process, but we parents need to understand that acceptance by peers is now more urgent for our teenager than acceptance by us. And that's not because he no longer likes us (no matter what he says); it's because he's feeling a natural desire to belong with other people.

Goal 2: Power

Your teen has grown physically from a child into a more powerful being who is now not only bigger and stronger, but capable of reproducing other human beings. She is intellectually more powerful, able to consider "what might be" as opposed to "what is." It's natural for her to want to use these new skills in new ways. She may become critical of everything (including Mom and Dad), basking in the power her new intelligence gives her. In fact, she may find herself arguing for arguing's sake, just to enjoy her increased ability.

Although teens who are trying out their new-found power are frustrating to live with, their experiments in empowerment are an important part of the transition from dependence to independence. Remember, if your teen is to successfully become an independent adult, she must have the power to leave you when the time is right.

Goal 3: Protection

All people have a desire to protect themselves, both physically and emotionally. As your teen's personal identity takes shape, he will go to great lengths to protect his sense of self. He wants to define himself as his own person, independent of you. He may perceive any attempts to limit behavior and freedom as attacks on his self-image. He will almost certainly resent signs of disrespect and react with hostility.

Remember, the goal of protection is normal for a teen. Don't force him to rebel against your values in order to protect his emerging identity. Let him assert himself in safe ways—through his choice of music, clothing, and hair style, for example—so he does not feel compelled to assert himself in unsafe ways, such as drug abuse. You can also respect his point of view, even when you disagree. Give him the message that "You don't have to be just like me; you just have to abide by certain rules."

Goal 4: Withdrawal

The development of one's own identity leads most teens to
withdraw into their own space. Spending more time alone in their
bedrooms is usually normal behavior for teenagers. They need
time and privacy to sort out all the changes they're experiencing,
to understand their new world and their place in it. Even though
you may feel like your teen's rejection of you is a personal affront,
remember that all teens strive for their own personal space as a
way of defining themselves. For the most part, you should give
them their privacy. But, there are two exceptions: 1) if you
suspect drug or alcohol use; and 2) if your teen is depressed. Too
much withdrawal can be a signal that one of these major problems
exists. In that case, you should get involved. We'll discuss how to
determine when to step in and when to let things alone a little later
in the chapter.

Goal 5: Challenge

The four goals we have discussed begin early in childhood and
continue throughout your teen's life. But the fifth goal—
challenge—seems to be strongest during adolescence. Your teen's
desire to test his skill and courage against an obstacle is one way
he measures how well he is doing on his journey from dependence
to independence. It is a natural, age-old part of growing up. In
fact, in many cultures teens have to endure a structured, traditional
challenge to mark the transition from child to adult. Because few
teens in our culture must face the challenge of literal survival
(thankfully), many create their own challenges by challenging *you*.
Again, this is perfectly normal.

Positive and Negative Approaches to the Five Goals

I hope you are feeling a little better around about now. After all, we have just learned that much of your teen's behavior is her way of reaching certain goals, *not* a personal attack against you. But that doesn't mean that all teenage behavior is acceptable. Teens can reach their goals through either positive or negative approaches. Teens with high self-esteem and courage will more often choose a positive approach to achieving their goals. Discouraged teens with lower self-esteem will more likely turn to easier, negative approaches. It is important to remember that these kids are neither inherently good nor bad. Based on their beliefs about themselves and the world and their level of courage, they choose good or bad *behavior* to reach their goals.

Positive Approach	Teen's Goal	Negative Approach
Contributing/Cooperating	Contact/Belonging	Undue Attention-Seeking
Independence	Power	Rebellion
Assertiveness/Forgiveness	Protection	Revenge
Appropriate Avoidance	Withdrawal	Undue Avoidance
Safe Adventures	Challenge	Thrill-Seeking

Negative and Positive Approaches: Contact/Belonging

Raul's parents were divorced, and he didn't see his father anymore. His mom worked long hours making ends meet, so he didn't see much of her either. Raul didn't have any close friends at school. So when members of the local gang started hinting that he might "get in" if he wanted, Raul was excited. He saw an opportunity to be somebody and to have friends. The other boys talked about being "family." Here was a chance to belong to a group whose members cared about and stood up for each other. Raul was so eager to join that he ignored the whispered stories of violent activities associated with these boys.

Keri had no interest in joining the trouble-making group at her school. She knew that they broke the law, and that several of them were serving time in a juvenile correctional facility. Plus, she had heard that getting in a gang was easy, but that getting out could be dangerous. Besides, she had plenty of friends and played on the girls' soccer team. The team was her "gang."

Everyone enjoys the attention of others, but when teens use negative behavior to fit in, we call this "undue attention-seeking." Raul does not have a close family, good friends, or outside activities to help fulfill his need to belong, so he turns to the attentions of a gang. Keri, on the other hand, has good friends including those on her soccer team. She found a positive approach to belonging by contributing her skills and ideas in these groups.

Negative and Positive Approaches: Power

Daryl had looked forward to getting his driver's license since he was twelve. He had gotten his parents to take him to get a learner's permit the first day he had been eligible. His parents had been good teachers, helping Daryl understand the responsibility of driving as well helping him develop the skills to drive well. Now he had passed his test and received his license. As he drove off to school by himself for the first time, he felt an independence and freedom that was powerful.

Dawn, fifteen, was tired of her parents trying to "run my life," as she put it. One night she decided it was time to take matters into her own hands. When her mom and dad told her she couldn't go to the mall with her friends because she had to baby-sit her little sister, she told them "no way." She made sure she slammed the door on her way out. Enroute to the mall with her friends, Dawn felt an independence and freedom that was powerful.

Both Daryl and Dawn are experimenting with their new sense of power. Daryl, who has the self-esteem and courage to take the positive approach to independence, enjoys the freedom that comes with responsible behavior. Dawn has taken the negative approach to getting power. Her rebellion serves to gain her some temporary independence, but at a high price to her relationship with her parents.

Negative and Positive Approaches: Protection

Tina felt that her father was always on her case about something. His yelling and putting her down for her mistakes made her angry. She knew he would only punish her more. Finally, she gave up trying to please him. She wanted to get even, but didn't dare. She began sneaking out to spend more time with her boyfriend, Carl. When he pushed her to have sex, she thought, "Why not? Nobody else really cares about me." When Tina became pregnant, her father couldn't believe it. After all he had tried to do for her, this is how she had repaid him. He was devastated.

Yolanda's boyfriend was pressuring her to have sex. Although she really liked him, she knew she was not ready for that step. One night his high-pressure tactics were too much for Yolanda. "Look," she told him. "I really don't like it when you keep pushing me to do something that I've already told you I don't want to do. If you keep pushing me, we're going to have to stop seeing each other."

Both Tina and Yolanda are seeking to protect themselves from those who want them to do and be things that run counter to their emerging identities. Tina's lack of self-esteem and courage have led her to use the negative approach of revenge. She has been hurt by her dad and seeks to protect herself by hurting him back. Of course, she is unaware of these goals and approaches and just thinks that she got "carried up in a moment of passion." Yolanda also wants to protect herself, but because she has a stronger base of self-esteem and courage, plus a clear value system, she is able to protect herself by being assertive.

Negative and Positive Approaches: Withdrawal

Grant had always struggled with schoolwork. He had been diagnosed with Attention Deficit Disorder (ADD) as a child, but the extra tutorial help he received did not change his basic opinion of himself as a lousy student. His grades, and subsequently his efforts, continued to deteriorate in his sophomore year of high school, until his parents finally threw up their hands in defeat. They felt as helpless as he did. Shortly after his sixteenth birthday, Grant dropped out of school.

Tyrone also struggled with ADD, but he never saw himself as a failure because of it. His parents had explained to him that school work would be a challenge for him, but that many people with ADD actually had intellectual and emotional strengths that those without ADD often lacked. They helped him find biographies of Thomas Edison and other ADD success stories to help him see the special side of ADD. When Tyrone felt discouraged, he didn't give up. He lay on his bed, closed his eyes, and thought about Thomas Edison, who always had something encouraging to say.

Grant and Tyrone struggle with the same learning challenge, ADD. Grant became highly discouraged as a result and took the negative approach of avoidance to withdraw from the problem altogether. Dropping out of school was an act of surrender. He had given up on himself. Tyrone took a different approach. He used his time alone to motivate himself. He learned to find the strengths as well as the weaknesses in his abilities and to master the challenge of school.

Negative and Positive Approaches: Challenge

Diane was a self-proclaimed thrill-seeker. She loved the adrenaline rush that came from living life on the edge. Trying a new drug, having sex with a new guy, shoplifting—all these gave her a feeling of excitement that contrasted with the boredom of her home life. No one in Diane's family was much of a "joiner," and most evenings were spent in front of the television. Diane knew she drove her friends and parents crazy with worry sometimes, but they always got over it. Besides, nothing bad was going to happen to her. She was "smart."

Steve started dating Diane at the beginning of their junior year. He was attracted to her sense of adventure and free spirit from the start, but lately he was beginning to worry about her. Steve liked a good challenge, too, but he found plenty of adventure in sports. He had saved his money from a part-time job to buy a mountain bike. He loved getting out on weekends with a group that rode fast and hard. He was working on getting Diane to give it a try, but so far she'd rather do her own thing.

Diane has chosen the negative approach of thrill-seeking to meet her goal of challenge. The more dangerous the activity, the better she likes it. Bike helmets and safety procedures seem dull to her. Of course, she is heading for a huge fall of her own.

Steve chooses to channel his desire for challenge into skill-building and reasonable risk-taking activities such as biking and other sports. His attempts to help Diane do the same may eventually work out, but the likelihood is that she will soon find him too dull and will move on. The challenge for Steve will be to find a friend who is a "free spirit" without being reckless.

How to Determine a Teen's Goal

Parents do not usually know the real goals behind teen misbehavior. Often, the discipline they choose actually makes the problem worse by rewarding or "paying off" the teen. (For example, imagine that your teen is rebellious because he wants more power over his relationship with you. If you spend a lot of time arguing with him, you are actually "rewarding" or "paying off" his negative approach because you are letting him dictate your actions—he is now powerful because he can make you angry.)   If you know your teen's goal, however, you can guide her toward the positive approach to getting it.

At the beginning of this chapter, a fourteen-year-old named Jason insisted on getting a tattoo against his parents' wishes. Which of the five goals do you think was driving his behavior?

If you're having a hard time picking just one goal, you're catching on. Jason could have gotten the tattoo because:

- He wants to fit in with a group at school (contact/belonging).
- He wants to show the world that he can do anything with his body that he wants (power).
- He wants to get even with his parents for a real or perceived injustice (protection).
- He wants to avoid fitting in with the "preppie" group at his school (withdrawal).
- He wants to see if he can endure the pain of tattooing and to challenge conventional fashion (challenge).

Look at two factors when trying to determine your teen's goal:

① your own feeling during a conflict

② the teen's response when you try to correct his misbehavior

In the case of Jason, his parents feel angry at him for getting the tattoo, and he refuses to have it removed (and threatens to get another one), so we can guess that Jason is trying to gain power by rebelling.

If we feel:	And the teen's response to correction is:	Then the negative approach is:	To the teen's goal of:
annoyed	stop, but start again very soon	undue attention-seeking	contact/belonging
angry	increase the misbehavior or give in only to fight again another day	rebellion	power
hurt	continue to hurt us or increase the misbehavior	revenge	protection
helpless	become passive/refuse to try	undue avoidance	withdrawal
unusually afraid	takes even more risks	thrill-seeking	challenge

Redirecting Our Teens' Behavior

Let's look more closely at five ways your teen could try to reach a goal through negative approaches, then look at how you can avoid paying off these approaches and begin redirecting him toward positive behavior.

1. Undue Attention-Seeking (Contact/Belonging)

The teen who seeks to belong through undue attention-seeking mistakenly thinks that she must be the center of attention in order to belong. While young children will do things to get this attention from *parents*, teens usually prefer the attention of *peers*. They may become class clowns or notorious troublemakers in their effort to stay in the limelight.

Sibling rivalry is one way for your teen to get "undue attention" from you.

While peers may encourage such negative behavior, adults usually feel annoyed or irritated. When confronted by an adult, a teen will usually stop his negative behavior for a while, but then continue again soon. This makes sense: consider that the teen's goal is contact, and that by confronting the teen we give him that contact. This satisfies his desire for attention for awhile, but not for long.

We parents play into the hands of teens seeking attention when we remind, nag, coax, complain, give lectures, scold, and otherwise stay in contact with teens when they irritate us.

What can you do differently?

- Do the unexpected. Break the pattern that your teen has come to expect and avoid the pay-offs which keep your teen misbehaving. In the case of undue attention-seeking, act more and talk less.
- Help your teen achieve the recognition and contact she wants by playing a useful role. Help find meaningful ways for her to contribute to the family while ignoring some of her unproductive attention-getting behavior.
- When you must discipline, briefly confront her with an "I" message or a logical consequence. (These techniques will be presented in Chapter 4.)

$+$

When Raul joined a gang, his mother became very concerned. She constantly lectured him about the dangers. She still worked long hours, but now she made time to talk to him. She confronted him whenever they were together. Raul was getting undue attention from his mother for doing something that she didn't approve of. Her lecturing, although unpleasant, was the most contact he had had with her in years.

When Mother realized that her nagging was just another "pay off" for Raul's negative behavior, she decided to change tactics. Realizing that Raul's goal was to belong, she spoke to the youth director at her church. Raul had always enjoyed basketball but hadn't played much in the last couple of years. She managed to get him to join a church league and even made time to take him to some of the games. After the games, she made him a special dinner, which the two enjoyed together. In this way, she began to loosen the hold Raul's gang had on him. She felt confident that in time Raul would lose interest in the gang altogether.

(2.) Rebellion (Power)

Rebellion is the most common of the five negative approaches, and the one that causes the most conflict in families and schools throughout the world. The teen who becomes discouraged trying to gain power in positive ways can easily find power through rebellion. After all, the ability to say "no" is a very powerful one, as every two-year-old has learned.

If parents have an autocratic leadership style, their teen may justly feel that his natural movement toward independence has been wrongly stifled. A teen with strong self-esteem and courage will stand up to his parents and negotiate for more freedom. But if the teen is already discouraged and lacking self-esteem, he may simply rebel through negative behavior.

A rebellious teen is typically trying to gain power.

Rebellious teens mistakenly believe the only way they can achieve power is by controlling others, or at least by showing others they cannot be controlled by them.

You'll know you're in a power struggle when you get angry at your teen. When you express this anger—thereby joining in the power struggle and "rewarding" your teen's rebellion—your teen's response will probably be to struggle harder and misbehave more. When you argue, you are saying to your teen, "Look how powerful you are: You have made me angry and pulled me down to your level." Parents also pay-off rebellious behavior by giving in. That conveys the message, "Look how powerful your rebellion is: It has gotten you your way."

What can you do differently?

- Refuse to fight or give in, and you'll side-step the struggle for power.
- Communicate more confidence in your teen's ability to make decisions for himself. Let him make mistakes and experience the consequences . . . without lecturing or humiliating him.
- Set up family council meetings (Chapter 6) to involve the teen in making decisions that affect the whole family.
- Use the Family Enrichment Activities, communication skills, and methods of encouragement outlined in this book to begin winning a more cooperative relationship.
- When discipline is necessary, use logical consequences (Chapter 4) and active problem-solving (covered later in this chapter) rather than anger and punishment.

Dawn's parents concluded that yelling and grounding Dawn were only making matters worse. The more they tried to control her, the more she seemed to rebel. They stopped fighting but did not give in to her unreasonable demands. They asked Dawn to sit down and discuss the problem together. "You know, Dawn," they began, "it seems that the more we try to control you, the more you resent it. Maybe there's room for us to back off a little without giving up our responsibility as parents." Dawn was pleased that her parents were finally paying attention to her feelings. She agreed to try solving problems together.

Dawns parents' made sure they focused on her strengths and avoided the discouraging comments they had made in the past. With their daughter they came up with a list of guidelines about going to the mall and other places. They knew that there would be other power struggles, but everyone felt encouraged that they had taken an important first step.

3. Revenge (Protection)

When you punish or hurt your teen, his response may be to get revenge by hurting you back. Revenge is the negative approach to the goal of protection.

Power struggles can often escalate into revenge-taking, especially if a teenager feels that his parent has "won too many battles" or has hurt him in the process. He decides that the best form of protection is to hurt back. In response, parents hurt back by punishing, thus setting off an escalating revenge cycle.

You can never win this revenge war. All the teen has to do to hurt you is to fail. He can fail at school, with his peers, with drugs, or with unsafe sex. In extreme cases, he can fail at life by committing suicide.

What can you do differently?

- To help, you must stop the revenge cycle. Instead of stubbornly demanding that your teen change (which is what many of us have been taught to do), play the leadership role in the family and call a cease-fire.
- Remember that no child is born "bad" or "mean." When teens act in a bad or mean way, they are hurting inside. Do what you can to stop whatever is hurting the teen. If it is your behavior, take a new approach. If someone else is hurting her, support her while she handles it herself, or take more direct action if needed.
- Sometimes a vengeful teen has not been wronged, but is hurting because of her misconception about how life ought to work. In these cases a calm and firm manner will help.
- Finally, the skills discussed in Chapter 4 for handling a power struggle are also useful in redirecting a revenge-seeking teen.

＋

Tina's pregnancy had hurt her father fiercely. This is what she unconsciously wanted—for all the times he had hurt her. When he understood this, his instinct was to hurt her some more. He wanted to call her a "stupid slut" and throw her out of the house. But he rose above his anger and indignation, realizing that he had been as much a part of the problem as his daughter. Tina was surprised when he sat down with her and told her that, no matter what happened, she was his daughter. He loved her and wanted to help her through this.

4. Undue Avoidance (Withdrawal)

Most teenagers withdraw at times from friends and family into their own thoughts and feelings. This self-reflection may be anxiety-ridden and full of doubt, but it is a normal part of development. You'll know your teen has crossed the line into undue avoidance when his behavior becomes a substitute for facing life's problems.

Teenagers who become discouraged may sink so low in self-esteem that they give up trying. Their belief becomes, "I can't succeed, so I'll stop trying—then I can't fail." They develop an apathy and lack of motivation that often leave parents feeling helpless. Such teenagers may miss school, fail to complete assignments, or even drop out. Alcohol and other drugs may become a way for those teens to avoid the challenges that life poses and to find temporary relief from their own discouragement.

Time alone (withdrawal) is healthy for teens. But excessive time alone may signal that your teen has given up on life's challenges. This is when she needs your encouragement the most!

It is often our own perfectionism that begins a teen's long, slow slide into undue avoidance. When we focus excessively on mistakes, when nothing ever seems to be good enough for us, when all we talk about is his great "potential," our child may give up trying altogether. Once a teen has chosen this path, his parents often make the mistake of giving up on him. They write him off as a loser and stop making an effort to help. Or they yell and scream, humiliate, and punish. Either way they send the message that "You're not good enough for us." This confirms the teen's own evaluation of himself and so justifies his avoidance.

What can you do differently?

- Communicate to your teen that succeed or fail, win or lose, she is still your child, and you are glad of it. Your love is unconditional.
- Practice patience and give a lot of encouragement.
- Remind yourself that your teen is exaggerating her avoidance to gauge your reaction. She wants to see if the worst is true— if she is really as bad off as she thinks.
- Help your teen find tasks at which she can succeed, so that she can begin to change her image of herself as a loser.
- Help her to see that mistakes are for learning, and that failure is just a lesson on the road to success.

Tyrone had grown so discouraged with his school failure that he had dropped out. His parents had thrown up their hands in defeat, accepting that their son had lost his ambition. But after a talk with a counselor, they decided this should not be the end of the story for them or Tyrone. Maybe a break from school would do Tyrone some good. They sat down with him to discuss his future. Everyone agreed that Tyrone should take a job and work through the end of the semester and then reevaluate the situation. In the meantime, since he was no longer a student, he would be expected to help pay his own expenses. His parents expressed confidence that he would make a good life for himself whatever path he ultimately decided to take.

5. Thrill-Seeking (Challenge)

Excitement is to teens as comfort is to . . . uh . . . well . . . us. In fact, if it weren't for teens and preteens, there would be little need for roller coasters or horror movies. After years of development, teens are ready to challenge themselves physically, emotionally, intellectually, socially, and spiritually. When we do not offer them healthy ways to do this, they'll find plenty of unhealthy ways. Alcohol and drugs, sexual experimentation, reckless driving, and breaking the law can be thrilling alternatives to a teen who sees everyday life as bland. For teens who are also choosing undue avoidance, thrill-seeking may become the only thing they feel they are good at. "If I can't be the best student," the thinking sometimes goes, "then at least I can be the biggest druggie." Dangerous pursuits are entertaining and exciting.

You'll know your teen is using this approach if you're unusually afraid for your teen when he misbehaves, and if, when you discipline him, he responds by taking even more reckless risks.

Teens especially need challenges. If they aren't offered healthy challenges, they often turn to dangerous, thrill-seeking behavior.

You heighten the appeal of thrill-seeking when you are overprotective and do not allow your teen to take any chances. Teens have a legitimate need to test themselves. When you try to stifle such desire, it often becomes stronger. Parents also err by reacting with anger and outrage when they find teens drinking or engaging in other harmful thrill-seeking behavior. This response often turns thrill-seeking into a power struggle. The teen now has two motivations to continue: the thrill itself and to show Mom and Dad that they can't run his life.

What can you do differently?

- Avoid power struggles by remaining firm and calm.
- Redirect your teen toward positive activities such as karate, cycling, rock climbing, white-water sports, team sports, a part-time job, a hobby, or adventure organizations such as scouting or Outward Bound.
- Help him enjoy vicarious thrills by taking him to ball games.
- Double the benefits by learning something together.
- Of course, you'll want to confront and discipline reckless behavior, and we will discuss this in detail later, but let's be more creative in our society by finding ways to help teens challenge themselves. This will eliminate much of the problem.

Diane was into the thrill-seeking of drugs, sex, and shoplifting. Danger gave her a sense of mastery and excitement that she couldn't get anywhere else. Her boyfriend, Steve, had tried to get her to channel this desire into mountain biking, but she wasn't interested. After they broke up, she turned to even more dangerous activities. One night, while high with some friends, she got arrested for shoplifting. Fortunately for her, her parents and the judge helped her get into a drug treatment program where she began to look at the consequences of her life. Family therapy was part of the process, as her parents discovered ways to help her build her self-esteem and courage.

Identifying the Negative Approach

Write down a recent conflict that you had with one of your teens, including what happened, what you said, and what he said._____

_____

_____

_____

_____

_____

How did you feel during the exchange (irritated, angry, hurt, hopeless, afraid)?_____

_____

_____

_____

How did your teen respond to your attempts to correct him?_____

_____

_____

_____

Using the chart on page 102, what was your teen's negative approach (undue attention-seeking, rebellion, revenge, undue avoidance, thrill-seeking)?_____

_____

_____

_____

What was your teen's basic goal (contact/belonging, power, protection, withdrawal, challenge)?

_____

How did you pay off this negative approach by helping your teen reach his goal?_____

_____

_____

_____

Problem-Prevention Talks

Anticipating problems before they happen can ease family tension, possibly even preventing a dangerous situation for your teen.

All families have problems. The main difference between families that function well and families that do not is their ability to solve those problems effectively, before they escalate out of control. The same is true for teens. The main difference between teens caught in failure cycles and those in success cycles is their ability to work productively on their problems, often with the help of a parent or other adult.

The old line about an ounce of prevention being worth a pound of cure applies completely when parenting teens. Many of the problems parents have with their teens could be avoided if everyone would take time to sit down and discuss the situation beforehand. When parents anticipate problems and establish guidelines ahead of time, teens are more likely to choose positive behavior. A problem prevention talk will also discourage your teen's "act now, ask questions later" approach to gaining permission. And teenagers are less likely to resist guidelines that they helped develop.

Problem prevention is not about laying down the law or telling your children about your guidelines. It's about discussing potential problems before they happen and deciding together on guidelines that will help prevent them. Although you and your teen will make some decisions jointly, you will have certain points that are not negotiable. This is part of your responsibility as a parent. You can still involve your teen by being flexible within those limits. The result of such a discussion will be clear guidelines about what you expect of your teen and the consequences for violating those guidelines.

To have a successful problem prevention talk, follow five general steps. As with all of the skills in this book, use these steps as guidelines rather than absolute rules:

1. Identify potential problems and risks.

2. Share your thoughts and feelings about these problems and acknowledge your teen's thoughts and feelings.

3. Generate guidelines through brainstorming and negotiation (within limits you can live with).

4. Decide on logical consequences for violating the guidelines (if necessary).

5. Follow up to ensure that guidelines were followed and to enforce the consequences (if necessary).

Examples of areas in which problem-prevention talks can be helpful include:

- schoolwork
- dating
- going to parties
- spending the night out
- choosing friends
- using the car

Let's look at the five steps more closely, with the use of the car as an example.

Step 1.

Identify potential problems and risks.

Think about the questions relating to the topic and anticipate where problems might occur.

- When will the teen get to use the car?
- Who pays for gas, insurance, and repairs?
- What does the teen need to know in case of an accident, such as insurance policy procedures?
- Does the teen know how to change a flat tire?
- Does the teen know not to hitchhike if the car breaks down? (Many teens are abducted and killed while hitchhiking each year.)
- Does the teen know the law regarding seat belts?
- Who may drive the car or ride in it?
- Is your teen aware of the grave dangers of driving after drinking?
- What should your teen do if he discovers that someone he is driving has alcohol or other drugs?
- What are the consequences if the teen does not follow the guidelines?

Step 2.

Share your thoughts and feelings about these problems and acknowledge your teen's thoughts and feelings.

For example, you may say, "My number-one concern is for your safety, and anything that we agree on has to be safe." Your teen may say, "Okay, but I really want to be able to use the car on Friday nights to go to the football games." Freedom of expression is a hallmark of Active Parenting, just as it is the foundation of life in a democratic society.

Step 3.

Generate guidelines through brainstorming and negotiation (within limits you can live with).

Your goal is to reach decisions that everyone can live with. These decisions may not be anyone's first choice. For example, Dad may want Son to buy all of his own gas. Mom may think that Son shouldn't have to pay for any. Son may not know what to think because he doesn't know if he can afford gas. Ultimately, they may decide that the teen should get a small gas allowance each week. There are lots of possibilities, though, and when you focus on finding solutions that satisfy everyone (rather than on winning arguments), you can really go far. But don't forget that you are still the parent, and that some of your concerns, such as no drinking and driving, can't be negotiated.

Step 4.

Decide on logical consequences for violating the guidelines (if necessary).

We will discuss logical consequences in detail in the next chapter. We use it here to mean establishing beforehand what will happen if the teen breaks an agreement. For example, the first time your daughter breaks an agreement about using the car, she might lose the car for a week. More serious violations, such as drinking and driving, might mean she cannot use the car for a longer period. Establish these consequences during your prevention talk.

Step 5.

Follow up to ensure that guidelines were followed and to enforce consequences (if necessary).

Enforcing a guideline, such as a curfew, is critical. How much you monitor your teen should be based on your teen's track record of reliability.

Be aware of your teen's behavior and whether he is keeping the agreements. If you want guidelines to work, you must enforce them. It's that simple. For example, if you want to enforce the no-drinking-and-driving guideline, you must be awake when your teen comes home at night to see if he's been drinking.

How much you follow up and monitor your teen is a matter of trust. Teens who always live by their agreements can be trusted more and do not need as much follow-up. But teens who break their agreements need regular follow-up until they establish a new track record of reliability. Be straight with your teen about this, and don't be intimidated by the old, "Don't you trust me?" routine. The answer to this is, "I trust you as far as your behavior shows me I should." If your teen has not consistently kept agreements, you can add, "Right now, because you broke curfew by forty-five minutes last Saturday without calling, I think I need to follow up a little more closely for a while."

Prevention Talk

Choose a situation in which your teen might do something you'd like to prevent (use of the car, dating, spending the night out, being left home alone). Write down the situation.

_____

_____

List the specific aspects of the situation that you and your teen will want to discuss:

_____

_____

After your talk, check which of the five steps you completed:

_____ Step 1: Identify potential problems and risks.
_____ Step 2: Share your thoughts and feelings about these problems and acknowledge your
                 teen's thoughts and feelings.
_____ Step 3: Generate guidelines through brainstorming and negotiation (within limits you
                 can live with).
_____ Step 4: Decide on logical consequences for violating the guidelines (if necessary).
_____ Step 5: Follow up to ensure guidelines were followed and to enforce consequences
                 (if necessary).

What did you like about how your talk went?

_____

_____

What will you do differently next time?

_____

_____

Do you think your talk helped prevent any problems? If so, what?

_____

_____

If problems occurred, did you follow through with logical consequences? If so, how did it go?

_____

_____

Who Owns the Problem?

Despite our best efforts at prevention, problems happen. Handling problems effectively requires the use of discipline and/or support. To determine which, you first need to figure out who *owns* the problem. In other words, who has the responsibility and authority to decide on the solution. It is either you, your teen, or in some cases, both.

What do I mean by owning the problem? Autocratic parents tend to act as if all problems were theirs, and that it is they who must always decide what should be done. These parents give teens too little freedom to solve their own problems. Permissive parents tend to act as if their teens should be responsible for all problems. These parents provide too little discipline and support.

Active parents understand that some problems belong to their teens, not them. In these cases, the teen should be free to decide how he will handle the problem. The parent's role is to offer *support*, not tell her teen what to do. The active parent also understands that the *parent* owns some problems. That's when *discipline* is needed. In some situations, responsibility should be shared by the parent and teen until the teen is able to handle the problem for herself.

You can usually determine who owns the problem by asking these questions:

1. Who is directly affected by the problem behavior?

2. Who is raising the issue or making the complaint?

3. Whose goals are being blocked? By this we mean: Who is not getting what they want?

Let's see some examples to help clarify this concept.

Situation	Who owns the problem?	Why?
Teen drives the car into the garage too fast.	Parent	It's the parent's responsibility to teach teens to drive safely.
Teen complains about her younger sister going into her room without getting permission.	Teen	Siblings have the right to have relationships with each other without parents involved. They need to learn to relate to each other on their own.
Teen forgets to do his family chore.	Parent	This affects everyone in the family, including the parents.
Teen doesn't come home until very late.	Parent	Parents have a responsibility to supervise their teens. This goal has been blocked by the teen's action.
Teen complains that her teacher gave her an unfair grade.	Teen	Schoolwork is the teen's responsibility. Her goal to do well in school has been blocked.
Teen is not keeping up with schoolwork.	Shared	Although schoolwork is the teen's responsibility, parents have a right to get involved until the teen shows he is willing to handle this responsibility himself.

Let's summarize what we have covered about preventing problems.

1. First, work to prevent problems through problem-prevention talks.
2. When a problem occurs, determine who owns it.
3. If the parent owns the problem, use discipline skills. If the teen owns the problem, use support skills. If the problem is shared, use discipline and support skills.

We will be covering these important discipline and support skills in the final three chapters. And of course, no matter who owns the problem, always look for opportunities to encourage, encourage, encourage.

Drugs, Sexuality, and Violence: Educate Your Teen

Lessons from the Titanic

On April 10, 1912 the Titanic left England for New York on its maiden voyage. By all accounts, it was the safest ship ever built. Only five days after embarking, an officer on the bridge saw an iceberg looming ahead in the Titanic's path. He had plenty of time to shut off the engines, steer far around the iceberg, and avoid the wreck. However, he mistakenly thought that he could save time by steering around just the tip of the iceberg with the engines still on. Instead, the Titanic struck the iceberg underwater and sank to the bottom of the ocean. The officer's mistake cost him his life as well as the lives of 1,523 others who went down with the ship.

Approximately seven-eighths of an iceberg is under the water. The officer steered around the smaller portion of the iceberg that was visible, but he failed to consider the huge width of the underwater portion, which ripped through the Titanic's hull like a can opener.

Many modern dangers teens face are like icebergs. Young men and women often think they know the risks of such ventures as drinking, drug use, sex, and criminal activity. They also mistakenly believe that they can steer around those risks and face challenges unharmed. However, like the officer on the Titanic, they often fail to see the bulk of the danger —addiction, STDs, pregnancy (and parenting), prison, death. Like the Titanic, they may have plenty of ballast to stay afloat in a storm, but one mistake in judgement can be deadly. Part of our jobs as parents is to help teach them about the risks and slow down their engines.

Ten Prevention Strategies for Parents:

Strategy #2. Educate your teens about the risks of drugs, sexuality, and violence.

The best way to know if your teen is getting accurate information about issues like the dangers of drug use is to provide the information yourself.

Teens get a lot of information about drugs, sexuality and violence from other teens. Unfortunately, much of this "street" information is either inaccurate or one-sided. Teens often emphasize the exciting aspects of these behaviors while downplaying or entirely ignoring the risks. To help remedy this information bias, many schools have instituted programs to help inform teens about the real dangers involved with substance use, sexual behavior, and violence.

If you are fortunate enough to have such a program in your school, find out exactly what the program is teaching. Besides making sure that the program fits with your own value system, you will probably learn useful information that you can then reinforce in conversations with your teen. Whether your school has such a program or not, it is important for you to be part of the educational process. Rather than having one long talk on these subjects, I recommend short but frequent discussions about these topics with your teen. This creates an open line of communication that can be extremely valuable as your teen meets challenging situations. As you engage your teen in these talks, keep the following points in mind:

Be prepared. To be convincing, you need more than emotion. You need facts. Know the harmful effects of drugs, including nicotine, alcohol, and marijuana, which many teens mistakenly think are harmless. Know the risks involved in sexual activity and the potential for violence in your community. If your school has programs in any of these areas, get involved. At the very least look at the materials so you can use the information in discussions with your teens. You can get information through the sources listed in appendix D.

Don't get hooked into an argument. If you become overbearing or disrespectful during these discussions, you give your teen a reason to rebel. Even teens who initially resist the facts may consider them later.

Invite your teen's input. Ask your teen for his view on the topic to see what information he can share. Keep the tone friendly. This is not a lecture, but a discussion. If you decide that you need to do more research, ask your teen to help gather more information about a topic.

Come from caring, not authority. You will influence your teen more by talking in terms of caring about your teen's well-being than by dictating and demanding obedience. You can always say, "Do you have any idea how much I love you and how much that makes me care about your health and safety?"

Cover many topics in your discussions. The following list can help you begin to plan. Of course, your own values will influence what you choose to talk about, especially in the area of sexuality. So use this outline as a starting place only.

Tobacco, alcohol, and other drugs

- Specific drugs, their effects and risks (including nicotine, alcohol, and marijuana)

- The physical, psychological, and social effects of using any drug

- The consequences of breaking the law

- The chance of other risky behavior while under the influence of a drug (for example, auto accidents)

Sexuality

- The reproductive process. (Don't assume they know everything.) Birth control. Whether you believe in abstinence, natural family planning, or methods such as condoms or pills, it is important that your teen be aware of the risks and benefits of each.

- Sexually Transmitted Diseases (STDs). AIDS is the biggest sexual risk facing teens today, yet most teens act as if they are immune. Teens should also know about herpes, syphilis, gonorrhea, chlamydia, venereal warts, and other STDs, as these are also very dangerous.

Violence

- Stranger danger. Which situations leave a teen vulnerable to rape, abduction, or other violence by a stranger? What can someone do to reduce these risks?

- Fighting. How do conflicts grow into fights? What are the risks? What could your teen do instead of fighting? If your teen is on the sidelines, how should he react?

- Date violence. (Fifteen percent of fourteen- to seventeen-year-old girls report that someone they were dating tried to force them to have sex with them. Forty percent report knowing someone who has been hit or beaten by a boyfriend). Discuss with your sons and daughters why boys hurt girls. Emphasize that physical force is wrong. Discuss self-esteem and mutual respect.

Let your teens know that no one should pressure them into doing something they're not ready for. Teach your teen that "no" means "no."

You may want to discuss many other topics during these talks. Use articles, books, and tapes to help you present the information. You and your teens can watch or read something together or separately, then talk about it afterwards. The following dialogue is an example of how a talk about AIDS might go between a parent and a teen:

125

Father: You've probably heard a lot about AIDS. I thought we should first talk about it ourselves. First of all, how much do you know about AIDS?

Josh: Why do you think I need to know about that?

Father: Well, there are a lot of things teenagers need to know about. This is just one of them.

Josh: Well, I know that AIDS is a disease that can kill you. That it has to do with the immune system. And that you can get it from having sex with a gay guy.

Father: Well, that's partially right. It is a disease that affects the body's immune system. In fact, the acronym AIDS stands for Acquired Immune Deficiency Syndrome. In other words, it attacks the body's immune system, leaving the person helpless to fight off diseases. People who get AIDS eventually die from some other disease because their bodies can't fight it off any more.

Josh: Yeah, I remember now. It sort of takes away their defenses.

Father: Exactly. And you're right about it being sexually transmitted. Because the AIDS virus is carried in blood and semen, most people who get AIDS get it from sexual intercourse. But some people have gotten AIDS from blood transfusions, although this is more rare because people are testing blood better than they used to. Also, some drug users get it from sharing needles.

Josh: Yeah, I saw that on a movie one time. This guy got AIDS from shooting up with a needle that a guy with AIDS had used.

Father: Right. The needle was infected. But there is one more thing that you're a little bit off on.

Josh: What's that?

Father: People don't get AIDS only from gays. In fact, the AIDS virus doesn't know a gay person from a straight person from a bisexual person. All it knows is that it can be transmitted through blood and semen, which means that it can also be carried through regular heterosexual intercourse.

Josh: Yeah, but I heard it's really rare to get it from a girl.

Father: I'm afraid that's no longer true.

Josh: Really? Well, how can you keep from getting it?

Father: The only sure way to keep from getting AIDS is not to have sex.

Josh: I'm supposed to never have sex?

Father: Well, it doesn't have to be quite that drastic. If you wait until you get married, and you're sure your partner doesn't have AIDS, and if the two of you are faithful during your marriage, then you can be 100 percent sure that you can be as sexual as you want to be and not get AIDS.

Josh: Can't you use a condom or something like that?

Father: Probably. If you use them correctly, they're supposed to prevent AIDS in most cases. But they're not 100 percent safe.

Josh: Well, if I ever had sex before getting married, I think I'd use one.

Father: Well, I hope you decide to wait until you're married. But if you don't, I'm real glad to hear you say that. In fact, I'd say that anybody who has sex these days without a condom is risking their lives.

127

Josh: Does everyone who gets AIDS die?

Father: They're working on finding a cure. But so far, that's pretty much true. Now, let's talk a little about why it's a good idea not to rush into having sex while you're a teenager . . .

Your teen is more apt to listen if your motivation is from caring, not dictating.

Family Enrichment Activity: Taking Time for Fun

Taking time for fun today builds memories you can recount years from now.

It's easier to like someone you have fun with. However, often we forget about the fun part of being a family when our schedules are so busy and when so much of our time together is spent in power struggles. Enjoyable shared activities help break negative parent-child cycles and enhance positive ones.

Our Family Enrichment Activity for this chapter is to take the time to do something fun with your teen. It can be as brief as ten minutes or as long as an all-day outing. The key is to make it something your teen enjoys. For example:

- throw a ball or shoot baskets
- bake a fancy desert
- play a game together
- go on an outing

To get the most out of this activity:

- Find something that you both enjoy.
- Ask for suggestions from your teen, but have some ideas of your own.
- Keep it fun! Do not use this time for confrontation.
- Record your experiences on the following chart.

Taking Time for Fun

Remember When . . .

Think about something fun you enjoyed doing with your parents when you were a teenager. Close your eyes for a moment and visualize the experience.

What was the fun activity that you and your parent shared?_____
_____
_____

How did you feel about your parent at that moment?_____
_____
_____

How did you feel about yourself?_____
_____
_____

Progress Chart

As you take time for fun with each of your teens, record the experience below.

1. Teen's name_____What did you do?_____
How did it go?_____

2. Teen's name_____What did you do?_____
How did it go?_____

3. Teen's name_____What did you do?_____
How did it go?_____

4. Teen's name_____What did you do?_____
How did it go?_____

5. Teen's name_____What did you do?_____
How did it go?_____

Chapter 3

Home Activities

Before you read farther, take the time to complete the following activities so you can practice what you've just learned.

1. Re-read any part of Chapter 3 that you want to review.
2. Observe your teen's behavior to achieve goals and how you may unintentionally pay off both positive and negative approaches to those goals.
3. Have a problem-prevention talk with your teen.
4. Complete the Taking Time for Fun chart on page 130.

Responsibility and Discipline

Responsibility Case Studies

Karen, fifteen, liked a boy at school her parents were convinced was "bad news." He had not done anything wrong that her parents knew about, but the way he dressed ("that earring!") was enough to convince them that he was not suitable for their daughter. After he brought Karen home an hour after curfew one night, both of them with alcohol on their breath, Karen's parents got angry and forbade her to see him again. She protested they were being unfair, and a shouting match began. Karen defiantly stormed out, slamming the door behind her.

Devon, twelve, had little interest in doing the few chores his mom had given him. She fussed at him a little, then usually just gave up and did them herself. It was easier than reminding him a dozen times, she figured. It also bothered her if Devon's room remained for long in its messy state, especially when dirty dishes from the previous night's snacks were left lying around. Cleaning up after him was getting pretty annoying, especially since she worked full-time and was a single parent.

Lisa, fourteen, had become a lot more interested in socializing than in schoolwork during the past year, and her grades showed it. Her parents were constantly on her case, but it did little good. Lisa would study for a few minutes, then have to call a friend to

talk over a question. This inevitably led to a long telephone conversation about anything but the original question. When her parents asked her about her grades, Lisa complained that school was boring.

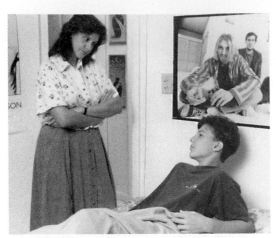

To help your teen learn responsibility, do not do for your teen on a regular basis what he can do for himself (like getting up on time for school).

What Is Responsibility?

Most parents would agree that the teens in the above situations are not behaving responsibly. But what does the term "responsible" really mean? For parents, the word means three things:

- accepting your obligations
- knowing the difference between right and wrong
- accepting accountability for your actions

Accepting Your Obligations

There are times in all of our lives when we would rather not do something we feel obligated to do. Responsible parenthood, for instance, is filled with times when we sacrifice our own immediate desires for long-term benefits for our families. Helping our teens understand the need for self-sacrifice is part of teaching them responsibility. When Devon's mother let him out of doing his chores, she missed an opportunity to teach him responsibility. The same is true when a parent lets a teenager out of going to a family wedding because the teen complains "Why do I have to go?" We can calmly explain to our teens that meeting our obligations comes before immediate pleasures. We can empathize with them when they have to pass up an invitation to go to a party because they have a prior commitment to perform in a chorus presentation. We can let them know that it takes courage to pass up some of the fun stuff in life, but that it will pay off in the long run.

Knowing the Difference between Right and Wrong

Helping our teens learn the difference between right and wrong is part of our jobs as parents. As our teens earn the freedom to choose, they also take on the responsibility to determine what is right. This is not always easy. For example, most adults would readily agree that it is right to obey the law, and that we should teach our children to do so. Yet when Dr. Martin Luther King, Jr., broke the segregation laws of Alabama during the Civil Rights Movement, we recognized his actions as not only responsible, but also as moral and courageous. Over time, people came to discover that the laws were wrong, and Dr. King was right.

Taking time to talk with our teens about right and wrong in real-life situations is the best way to help them grapple with these difficult issues. Continuing to challenge our own beliefs as we expand our conceptions about right and wrong is also an act of responsibility and courage.

In the example of fifteen-year-old Karen, her parents had unfairly judged her boyfriend based on his looks. Bringing their daughter home an hour late for curfew and drinking were other matters, however, and they had a responsibility to deal with both teens about their behavior. Forbidding Karen from seeing her boyfriend again is not likely to be effective and will probably lead to more defiance. But this didn't make Karen's actions—storming out of the house—right either. Teens have an obligation to obey their parents in such situations, and leaving against their will was wrong.

Accepting Accountability for Your Actions

Accepting that what happens to you results from decisions you make is at the very core of responsibility.

Accepting that what happens to you results from decisions you make is at the very core of responsibility. As with everyone, it is much easier for teens to blame their problems on other people or circumstances, or just to make excuses. But doing so prevents them from learning to make better decisions in the future. After all, if it wasn't my fault, why should I think about what I could do differently next time?

For example, when Lisa's grades dropped because she was socializing too much and studying too little, she blamed it on her teachers for being boring. This thinking is not likely to help her improve her grades, since she can't control her teachers to make them more interesting. But what if she took responsibility and said to herself, "You know, there is a lot of boring stuff in those classes, but I want to do well in school, so I'd better study harder anyway. Maybe I can even make some study dates so it will be more fun." When teens accept responsibility for what happens to them, they learn to prevent or solve their own problems.

You can think of responsibility as a formula:

Responsibility = Choice + Consequences

This formula covers all three aspects of responsibility, since choices include the choice to meet or not meet one's obligations and the choice of right or wrong.

How can we help our teens develop responsibility? First, recognize that teens often avoid responsibility because of how they're treated when they confess their mistakes. Often their reward for taking responsibility is blame, discouragement, and sometimes punishment. Most people learn even as children that if they can make a good excuse or blame it on someone else, they can avoid being hurt for their mistakes and misbehaviors.

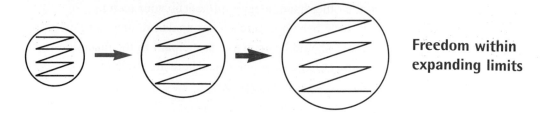

Freedom within expanding limits

The first step in helping your teen learn responsibility is to avoid hurting her when she makes a bad choice. Redirect her to make a better choice that will help her achieve her goal. Try not to discourage her further through put-downs, punishments, or other disrespectful actions.

To help your teen take responsibility without hurting her, you'll need discipline skills that are neither autocratic nor permissive. The active (authoritative) style of parenting is based on the concept of "freedom within limits." This means allowing your teen the freedom to make choices within limits that are appropriate for her age and level of responsibility. The better your teen handles her freedom of choice, the more freedom you allow her in the future. It's time to talk in detail about these authoritative discipline skills.

Active Discipline Skills

Discipline is from the Latin word, *disciplina*, meaning "to teach." We have already said that punishment does not teach, but instead produces rebellion and retaliation. Likewise rewards, although they may seem effective, lead to a "what's in it for me" attitude that is counter to the qualities of responsibility and cooperation you are trying to teach.

Neither reward nor punishment are effective discipline tools in the long run.

137

Discipline, on the other hand, ideally influences your teen to choose more positive behavior to reach her goals. It does not hurt or bribe. Your teen should be an active participant in the discipline process, not a subject to be manipulated. There are three main aspects to this active style of discipline:

- participation
- mutual respect
- focusing on the problem

Participation

What gives people power in a democracy? It's not the right to vote, since we actually vote on very few things. What gives us power is the first item on the Bill of Rights: freedom of speech. Democracy does not mean that we always get our way; it means that we always get our say. As long as we can say whatever we think (with only a few extreme exceptions), we can influence our leaders to make good decisions on our behalf. Our participation through freedom of speech gives us legitimate power. We don't need to rebel as long as we can speak our minds.

The same is true with teens. The more you can involve your teen in finding solutions to problems, the more likely he will feel committed to honoring these solutions and the less likely he will feel the need to rebel.

Mutual Respect

Democracy means that all people are created equal under the law. We've been working hard at this goal in this country, especially in your and my lifetime.

Our teens have grown up in this atmosphere of mutual respect in which people are very sensitive to signs of disrespect. They have come to expect respectful treatment. The days when parents could demand respect from their teens but speak disrespectfully to them in return are over—gone the way of segregation and other relics of our past. Today's parents must understand that, in the words of author Bernard Malamud, "Respect is what you have to have in order to get." *In other words, if you want your teen to treat you with respect, you must first be willing to treat her with respect.*

If you want your teen to treat you with respect, you must first be willing to treat her with respect.

Showing your teen respect means not yelling, cursing, calling him names, being sarcastic, or otherwise speaking to him in ways you would not want him to speak to you. And it means not letting him speak to *you* disrespectfully either. (Again, the concept is *mutual* respect.) But there are countless forms of more subtle respect and disrespect. For example, an overprotective parent who jumps in and solves a teen's problems before she has struggled to find a solution for herself is being disrespectful. A parent who always insists on doing what he wants and never compromising to do what the teen wants is also being disrespectful.

The first step in teaching your teen respect is to treat him respectfully. When you slip and treat him disrespectfully, catch yourself with a smile, apologize, and make amends.

Treating our teens in ways we wouldn't tolerate from them is disrespectful.

139

"I'm sorry I yelled at you, Ben. That wasn't very respectful. Let me try again more calmly to tell you why I was angry."

"I apologize for not calling to tell you I would be late. I know I expect you to let me know when you'll be late, so I should do the same."

When your teen treats you disrespectfully, you can treat his behavior as you would any other problem that you own and use one or more of the discipline skills presented in this chapter to help redirect him to more positive behavior.

Focusing on the Problem

Discipline can help solve problems and teach our teens responsibility. It can also escalate problems to another level. The third key to using discipline skills wisely is to keep your focus on the problem, not the teen. If your teen is talking to you disrespectfully, the problem is his behavior, not his personality. As we saw in Chapter 2, teens get tremendously discouraged when their personality is attacked. They resent it and will often find a way to retaliate.

It is much more respectful to say: "I don't like you talking to me that way. It is disrespectful," than it is to say: "You are so disrespectful."

The second response labels the teen's personality as disrespectful. But how do you change your basic personality? Such a statement says to the teen that there is something fundamentally wrong with him: You are disrespectful. It attacks his self-esteem, which usually makes teens want to misbehave in the future.

Stick to the problems, invite your teen to participate in finding a solution you both feel good about, treat your teen with respect, and you will find the following discipline skills to be amazingly effective.

Basic Discipline Methods

The first three methods of discipline we will discuss are an efficient place to start when you have a problem. Keep in mind that you should be only as assertive as you have to be to create change. We've presented them in the order of least firm to most firm. You should consider using them in that order, too. They are:

- Polite requests
- "I" messages
- Firm directions

Polite Requests

Not every problem or conflict requires a full-fledged discussion or firm discipline. Often, asking your teen politely is enough to influence him to change his behavior (especially if your relationship is already a positive one).

When your teen doesn't know what you want in a situation, the first step is to politely make your desires known through a request. For example, you have decided that you no longer want to pamper your teen by picking up the dirty dishes he leaves in the den. Your polite request might be, "Honey, from now on will you do me a favor and bring your dirty dishes to the sink when you're through with your snack?" If your teen agrees, be sure to add, "Thanks, that will be a big help."

This may seem so simple that it sounds ridiculous, but sometimes that's all teens need. Of course, you could wait until you're fed up with being a servant, hold it inside for another week to let it really boil, then burst out with, "I'm sick and tired of having to pick up your mess! What do you think I am, your servant? If you weren't so lazy and inconsiderate . . . ." However, this is not likely to produce responsibility, cooperation, or dishes in the sink.

If at first your teen does not comply with your polite requests, offer a friendly reminder: "Honey, I noticed you forgot to put your dishes in the sink. Please come get them."

"I" Messages

If your teenager repeatedly forgets to keep an agreement or is taking a negative approach to one of the five goals, you'll need a stronger message. "I" messages are firm and friendly communication that can produce surprisingly effective results. Psychologist Tom Gordon called them "I" messages in his pioneering program, Parent Effectiveness Training (P.E.T.), because they shift the emphasis from the teen (a traditional "you" message) to how the parent ("I") feels about the teen's behavior. "I" messages:

- allow you to say how you feel about your teen's behavior without blaming or labeling her.
- create a situation in which your teen is more likely to hear what you are saying because it is said in a respectful manner.
- tell your teen one result of her behavior (which is your feelings).
- give your teen clear information about what change in behavior you want.

When to Use an "I" Message

"I" messages are effective only when the parent owns the problem (when she has the responsibility and authority to decide on the solution).

Since "I" messages work best when delivered in a firm, calm tone of voice, avoid using them when you are too angry. Allow time for a cooling-off period, then approach your teen when you have regained control. If your teen's goal is power, an angry "I" message can easily make your teen want to rebel, especially if you say it aggressively rather than assertively.

How to Send an "I" Message

There are four parts to an "I" Message:

1. Name the behavior or situation you want changed.

Mom is firm when giving an "I" message, not angry. An angry tone often blocks communication.

As I noted when discussing encouragement in Chapter 2, it is important to separate the deed from the doer. Your teen is not bad; instead, you have a problem with something he is doing. By focusing on your teen's behavior, you avoid attacking his personality and self-esteem, and you reduce his defensiveness. Begin this part with: "I have a problem with . . ."

For example, "I have a problem with you coming home late."

143

2. Say how you feel about the situation.

Telling your teen your feelings without yelling and screaming still lets her know that you consider the problem serious. What are common parental feelings when teens misbehave? Would you guess anger? Although parents often use the word "angry" to describe their feelings, very often anger is only a mask for two other emotions: fear and hurt. Teens usually hear us better when we are expressing these emotions rather than anger because they are less threatening. "I feel concerned" or "I feel hurt" may come closer to describing how you really feel, as well as being more effective. This part of the "I" message begins with "I feel . . ."

For example, "I feel worried."

3. State your reason.

Nobody likes to be treated as if he or she were expected to be blindly obedient. If your teen is going to change what he is doing to please you, he'll want you to at least have a good reason. Give your teen a simple explanation about how his behavior is interfering with the needs of the situation. It can begin with: "because..."

For example, "because you may have been in an accident."

So far we have:

> I have a problem with you coming home late.
> I feel worried because you may have been in an accident.

4. Say what you want done.

You have already made a polite request or two, so now you are getting more assertive. This means letting your teen know exactly what you would like done. Remember, you'll get only what you ask for. This step can begin with "I want," "I would like," or "I expect."

For example, "I would like you to come home on time."

Putting this "I" message together we have:

> I have a problem with you coming home late.
> I feel worried because you may have been in an accident.
> I would like you to come home on time.

Making "I" Messages Stronger

Get agreement: "Will you please . . ."

You can make an "I" message even stronger by getting your teen to agree to the behavior that you want changed. You can do this after the "I" message by simply adding the question, "Will you do that?" and then not moving until you get a "yes." You can also change the last step of the "I" message from "I would like . . ." to "Will you please . . .?"

For example, "I have a problem with you coming home late. I feel worried because you may have been in an accident. Will you come home on time from now on?"

Establish a time frame: "When?"

Every parent of a teenager knows what it's like to get an agreement from his teen about doing something, then finding it is still not done hours later. The solution is to get your teen to say when he'll do it. In the above example, the parent indicated *when* by saying "from now on" (the next time the teen comes home and each time after that). Other times, it can be added right after the teen agrees to the request by simply asking, "When?"

Firm Directions

If your teen does not respond to a polite request or an "I" message, you can get firmer by giving a short, yet firm, direction to your teen.

Example:

"Home. On time. Tonight."

When you give firm directions, the fewer words you use the better. They make a big impact, and they're also easy for your teen to remember. Above all, avoid the temptation to lecture or explain yourself while your teen stands there ignoring you. Remember, the more you talk, the less they hear.

Basic Discipline Practice

Try writing a polite request, "I" message, and firm direction for the following problem: Your teenager has spoken to you disrespectfully after you have politely asked him or her to use different language.

Step 1. Try a polite request.

Please_____

_____.

Step 2. Imagine that your teen continues to speak to you rudely. Try an "I" message.

I have a problem with_____.

I feel_____

because_____

_____.

I would like (will you please)_____

_____.

Basic Discipline Practice *continued*

Step 3. What if your teen spoke to you politely for awhile, but then started speaking disrespectfully again? Use a firm direction._____

_____

Now write down a problem that you have had with one of your own teens. (Make sure you own this problem.) Write a polite request, an "I" message, and a firm direction you can use in this situation:

Step 1. Polite request

Please_____

_____.

Step 2. "I" message

I have a problem with_____.

I feel_____

because_____.

I would like (would you please)_____

_____.

Step 3. Firm directions_____

_____

Evaluation

How did your teen respond to each method?_____

_____

What did you like about how you delivered the discipline?_____

_____

Would might you do differently next time?_____

_____

_____

Advanced Discipline Methods

When basic discipline methods do not solve your problem, you can use two more structured skills that are stronger:

- Natural and Logical Consequences
- Active Problem-Solving

Natural Consequences

Remember that responsibility means accepting that what happens to you is a result of your choices.

Responsibility = Choice + Consequence

To teach your teen responsibility for her actions, you must give her the freedom to choose and let her experience the consequences of those choices. Teens learn a lot about what works and what doesn't from the consequences of their actions. We will discuss two types of consequences: natural and logical.

Natural consequences are what happen naturally (that is, without parents interfering) after teens choose to do or not do something.

Example:

- The natural consequence of not putting gas in the car is running out of gas.
- The natural consequence of oversleeping on a school day is being late for school.
- The natural consequence of leaving a bicycle outside may be that it gets rusty or that it is stolen.

Natural consequences are powerful teachers. They work well for parents because they allow them to act as a sympathetic third party, rather than the disciplinarian. To allow natural consequences to be effective, avoid two temptations:

1. to rescue (for example, drive him to school)
2. to say "I told you so." It's better to say, "Gee, honey, I know that's frustrating."

When You Can't Use Natural Consequences to Teach

There are three circumstances in which a responsible parent cannot allow Mother Nature to take her toll:

1. When the natural consequence may be dangerous. For example, the natural consequence of experimenting with drugs can be addiction or even death.

2. When the natural consequence is so far in the future that the teen is not concerned about the connection. For example, the natural consequence of not doing school work may be not graduating or fewer career choices.

3. When the natural consequence of a teen's behavior affects other people rather than the teen. For example, the teen returns your car with the gas gauge on empty, and you run out of gas. In such a situation, the parent owns the problem and must take action to prevent such natural consequences from occurring. Or, perhaps, you give your teen a bike you've worked hard to pay for, and she leaves it outside where it gets stolen. You may be angrier at losing the hard-earned bike than your teen is. In this case, allowing a natural consequence may not be your best discipline choice.

Logical Consequences

In cases in which you cannot rely on natural consequences, you'll need to set your own consequences to teach responsibility. We call these "logical" consequences because they are logically related to the misbehavior.

Logical consequences are the results that a parent deliberately chooses to show a teen what logically happens when he chooses to misbehave.

Examples:

- When Sean continually forgets to bring his dirty dishes into the kitchen after snacking in the den, he loses the privilege of taking food out of the kitchen.
- When Susan forgets to put gas in Mom's car when she borrows it, she is not allowed to use the car for a week.

Logical Consequences versus Punishment

Logical consequences are not the same thing as punishment, even though the teen won't like either. Some of the differences are:

Logical Consequences:

- are logically connected to the misbehavior.
- teach responsible behavior.
- are given in a firm and calm way.

Punishment:

- is an arbitrary retaliation for misbehavior.
- is intended to teach obedience.
- is often delivered with anger and resentment.

Guidelines for Using Logical Consequences

To be sure you're giving a logical consequence and not a punishment, follow these guidelines. They may seem like a lot to remember at first, but as you practice, they'll become second nature.

1. Ask your teen to help decide the consequence.
2. Put the consequence in the form of a choice
      either/or choice
      when/then choice.
3. Make sure the consequence is logically connected to the misbehavior.
4. Give choices you can live with.
5. Keep your tone firm and calm.
6. Give the choice one time, then enforce the consequence.
7. Expect testing (it may get worse before it gets better).
8. Allow your teen to try again after experiencing the consequence.

1. Ask your teen to help decide the consequences.

One way to show your teen respect is to ask for her help in deciding the consequence. You stand a much better chance that your teen will cooperate with you if you include her in the decision-making process. You'll also be surprised how often she comes up with choices and solutions that you wouldn't have thought of alone.

Example:

"Katherine, I still have a problem with you leaving your things all over the den. What do you think we can do to solve it?"

Even if your teen has no helpful suggestions or is uncooperative about finding a solution, it is important that you asked. Since you have invited the teen's participation, she will be less likely to think of you as a dictator and to rebel against you.

2. Put the consequence in the form of a choice.

Logical consequences should always be presented in the form of a choice. The teen can choose positive behavior with a naturally positive consequence, or she can choose to misbehave and have a logical consequence.

Try one of these types of choices:

- either/or choices: "Either _____ or _____. You decide."

- when/then choices: "When you have _____, then you may _____."

Examples of either-or choices:

Katherine leaves her stuff scattered around the den in the afternoon.
- Yes: "Katherine, either put your things away when you come home from school, or I'll put them in a box in the basement. You decide."
- No: "Katherine, put your things away or I'm going to throw them in a box in the basement!" (This choice makes the parent sound like an angry dictator.)

Calvin continually forgets to put his dirty clothes in the hamper.
- Yes: "Calvin, either put your dirty clothes in the hamper or wash them yourself. You decide."
- No: "Calvin, if you don't start putting your dirty clothes in the hamper, you're going to have to wash them yourself." (This doesn't even sound like a choice.)

Examples of when-then choices:

Maria has trouble getting her homework done but likes to watch TV.

- Yes: "Maria, when you have finished your homework, then you may turn on the TV."
- No: "Maria, if you do your homework, you may stay up a half-hour later tonight." (This is a reward, not a logical consequence, because it offers the teen a price for something she should be doing anyway.)

Tom is about to go to the swimming pool, but he has ignored his regular Saturday chore of mowing the lawn.

- Yes: "Tom, when you have mowed the lawn, then you may go swimming."
- No: "Tom, you may not go swimming until you have mowed the grass." (That doesn't sound like a choice.)

3. Make sure the consequences are really logical.

When you use logical consequences, don't be surprised if the misbehavior continues for awhile. Your teen is testing to see if you'll follow through.

No matter who comes up with the consequence, it won't work unless it is logically connected to the misbehavior. Your teen will be better able to see the justice of such consequences and may accept them without resentment. If the consequence is not really related to the teen's behavior, however, it will seem like a punishment.

Not Logical	Logical
"Either be home by 6 o'clock or lose your stereo for a week."	"Dinner is served at 7. Either be here on time or eat it cold, but at 7:30 we're clearing the table."
"Either limit your phone calls to fifteen minutes, or you're not going out on Saturday."	"Either limit your phone calls to fifteen minutes or give up a night using the phone each time you go over fifteen minutes."
"Finish your homework or you're grounded."	"When you finish your homework each weekday, you can go out that weekend." (This is logical if you establish a "work before play" philosophy in your family.)

4. Give choices you can live with.

There are many potential logical consequences for any given problem. To come up with one, you may want to brainstorm with other parents, your spouse, or your teen. But it's up to you to be sure the consequence is not only logical but also one you can accept. For example, if your teen continually forgets to put his dishes in the dishwasher, a choice might be: "Either put your dishes in the dishwasher or I will do it for you and charge you for my services."

However, if you know that doing your teen's dishes even for a price will drive you crazy, then don't give him this choice. If you get angry at your teen as you do his dishes, you haven't stayed true to your promise that he has a legitimate choice. You want to be content with your teen's choice—whichever one he makes. A better consequence might be: "Either put your dirty dishes in the dishwasher, or I will serve the next meal without dishes." Then be prepared to serve dinner "unusually."

5. Keep your tone firm and calm.

When you give a choice, and later when you enforce the consequence, you must remain both calm and firm. An angry tone of voice (the autocratic parent's pitfall) invites rebellion and a fight. On the other hand, a wishy-washy tone of voice (the permissive parent's pitfall) tells your teen that you don't really mean what you say, and it also invites rebellion. A firm and calm tone by an authority figure says, "I will treat you respectfully, but you are out of bounds here. My job is to help you learn to stay in bounds, and I plan to do my job."

6. Give the choice one time, then act.

Mom turns off the TV because the misbehavior continued. Her action teaches a clear lesson.

To teach your teen a lesson with a logical consequence, you must enforce it. If your teen continues to choose a negative approach (the misbehavior), then immediately follow through with the consequence. Do not give the choice a second time without putting the consequence into effect. Your teen must see that his choice results in a consequence. The lesson must be clear.

Michael Joyce has been given the choice of either leaving parties where alcohol or other drugs are present or losing the privilege of going to parties for a month. One night while he's at a party, his parents call the hosting parents to see how the party is going. The Joyces are alarmed to learn some teens are drinking beer, so they tell Michael to come home immediately. When he gets home, they talk to their son about the situation, calmly and firmly: "We appreciate the fact that you showed the good judgment not to be drinking yourself. However, since we agreed that you would leave parties with alcohol or drugs, and you chose to stay, you won't be able to go any more to parties for a month." The Joyces then decide that the next time Michael plans to go to a party, they will call the host's parents before the party starts to check on the alcohol policy.

7. Expect testing.

"When you have mowed the grass, then you may go over to your friend's house."

When you begin to redirect your teen's misbehavior from negative choices toward positive ones, expect her to continue to misbehave for awhile. In fact, expect that it may get worse before it gets better. Your teen is testing you to see if you will really do what you say you will do. If you consistently enforce the consequences, she will soon see that her testing isn't working and she'll change her behavior. After all, teens don't do what doesn't work. But don't get overly angry when your teen tests you—because they almost all will. Just enforce the consequence firmly and calmly.

8. Allow your teen to try again later.

Since you want your teen to learn from the consequences of his choice, you need to give him a chance to try again after he's experienced the logical consequence.

Example:

Sondra has agreed to do her chores on Saturday before going off with her friends. Saturday afternoon, her dad notices that she has gone without doing them. When she comes home he tells her: "I noticed that you didn't do your chores before you left today as we agreed. That means you will be staying home all day tomorrow to do them. You can try again next Saturday." Next week, Sondra leaves again without doing her chores. Dad tells her: "I think you'd better plan on spending next weekend at home, Sondra."

Using Logical Consequences

Look back at your "I" message on page 147. For that same problem, write down a logical consequence. Write in the space below one way that you might present the choices and consequences to your teen during the discussion of the problem:

_____

_____

If your "I" message was effective, then you didn't have to practice your logical consequence.

Think of another problem in which you can develop a logical consequence. Write down the problem here:

_____

_____

Using Logical Consequences *continued*

Now, write down a choice and a logical consequence that you could use:

_____

_____

Meet with your teen to discuss the problem, and use this logical consequence or another one that you developed with the teen.

Evaluation

What was your teen's response to the discussion?

_____

_____

What was his response to the logical consequence? Did he test you to see if you would follow

through?_____

_____

_____

If the consequence isn't working, do you think you need to stick with it longer, or change the

consequence to something else?_____

_____

_____

If the consequence isn't working, have you violated any of the guidelines for setting up logical

consequences? (Check page 151.)_____

_____

What do you like about the way you handled the use of logical consequences?

_____

_____

What will you do differently next time?

_____

_____

_____

Discipline Overview

1. Make a polite request.
2. Give an "I" message.
   I have a problem with . . . .
   I feel . . . because . . . .
   Will you please . . . ?
3. Give a firm direction.
4. Allow a natural consequence to happen. (or)
   Give a logical consequence. (or)
   Use active problem-solving.

Active Problem–Solving

If your teen is rebellious or revenge-oriented, sitting down together to solve problems may work better than logical consequences.

Some teens may resist logical consequences, especially if they're rebelling or seeking revenge. If you've tried using logical consequences correctly and your teen still sees them as punishment, try sitting down with your teen to solve the problem together. Yes, you still have the authority to provide logical consequences if necessary, but you may find that using the following approach will help the two of you change from conflict to teamwork. By approaching the problem together, there's a better chance your teen will see the sense of finding a solution, especially if the solution benefits him too. Plus, by involving him in solving problems, you are helping him develop responsibility.

There are five basic steps to active problem-solving. They're very similar to those in the problem-prevention talks presented in Chapter 3. You do not have to use them rigidly. Instead, think of them as guidelines to keep you on the right track:

Active Problem Solving

Step 1. Identify the problem.

Step 2. Share thoughts and feelings about the problem and acknowledge your teen's thoughts and feelings.

Step 3. Generate solutions and future guidelines through brainstorming and negotiation (within limits that you can live with).

Step 4. Decide on logical consequences if needed.

Step 5. Follow-up to make sure agreements were kept (and enforce logical consequences as necessary).

Step 1. Identify the problem.

It is important to begin by clearly stating the problem in terms of behavior. Avoid attacking your teen's personality.

For example, in the opening situation in which Karen defied her parents and left the house after they forbade her to do so, her parents might sit down with her and say something like this:

Mother: Karen, your dad and I feel pretty bad about what happened last night and want to talk with you about what we can all do to work this out.

Karen: You mean work it out so I don't see Damian anymore.

Mother: I don't know what the answer is at this point. I just think we need to reach a solution that we can all agree on. What do you see as the problem?

Karen: I think the problem is that you guys are trying to run my life. I'm old enough to see who I want to see.

Mother: Okay, that's one problem. Maybe we do try to control you too much.

Karen: Well, you can't stop me from seeing Damian.

Mother: I also think there is a problem with you leaving the house after curfew.

Karen: Yeah, I guess.

Step 2. Share thoughts and feelings about the problem and acknowledge your teen's thoughts and feelings.

Everyone should feel free to express his thoughts and feelings without fear of censorship or criticism. If you blame or act judgmental, you will succeed only in turning off your teen. On the other hand, if you genuinely try to understand her thoughts and feelings about the problem, you will gain an important ally in the problem-solving process. Let's return to our scenario.

Father: I guess you're saying that we treat you like a baby when it comes to boys.

Karen: Yeah. I'm not stupid, you know.

Father: No, you certainly aren't. I just worry about you, that's all. After all, I know what some guys are up to.

Karen: Well, Damian isn't like that. He's cool.

Father: You seem to think a lot of him.

Karen: Yeah.

Father: What is it about him you like?

Step 3. Generate solutions and future guidelines through brainstorming and negotiation (within limits that you can live with).

Think creatively to generate possible solutions. Discuss them with an open mind until you find one or more that everyone can agree on. You should be willing to negotiate so that everyone feels they get as well as give in order to reach an agreement. If you simply lay down the law, your teen will probably rebel and retaliate more. Again, the concept of freedom within limits is important. Don't cave in and give up your responsibility to supervise and monitor your teens.

Mother: I like Karen's idea: As long as she and Damian stay within the guidelines we all agree to about dating, including curfews and the no-use rule about tobacco, alcohol, and other drugs, we stop giving her a hard time about Damian.

Father: So, that means no more coming in an hour later than curfew.

Karen: I promise. But how about if I invite him in for awhile when we get back?

Mother: That's okay with me . . . within reason. I don't want to stumble on him leaving when I get up for breakfast.

Karen: Mooom!

Mother: I'm kidding, Karen. How about an hour after curfew in the den? Your dad and I will go to our room so you can have it to yourselves. That okay with you, dear?

Father: Yeah, sounds good to me. Karen?

Karen: Yeah . . . sounds cool.

Step 4. Decide on logical consequences if needed.

This guideline is somewhat tricky. For some teens, the trust you have shown them by negotiating an agreement in good faith will be blown if you now bring up what will happen if they break that faith. Other teens respond better if they already know the consequences for failing to keep an agreement. If you are unsure how your teen will respond, you might try first without discussing a logical consequence. If he fails to keep up his end of the agreement, go through the process again, adding the consequence this time. Another option is to come up with logical consequences for everyone, parents included. This keeps a sense of equality and fair play.

Mother: So, we've agreed to stay off your back about Damian. And to let him come over for an hour after curfew in the den. And you've agreed to abide by the dating guidelines we all set up. What happens if any of us fails to keep an agreement?

Karen: You mean you guys get a logical consequence too?

Father: Sure. Want to ground us?

Karen: Big deal. You guys stay home all the time anyway.

Father: Seriously, how about if we "rag on" Damian, as you say, I'll buy you guys two movie tickets?

Karen: Cool!

Mother: And if you break your agreement?

Karen: How about I won't see Damian for a week?

Mother: How about two weeks?

Karen: Okay, but you guys'll blow it first.

Father: We'll stick to the agreement if you will.

Step 5. Follow up to make sure agreements were kept (and enforce logical consequences as necessary).

You have to be willing to expend this time and energy. Otherwise, your teen will test you and discover he can get away with misbehavior. You must follow-up so that your words will continue to be taken seriously.

Follow up also gives you an opportunity to make adjustments in the agreement if they're needed. You can also use the time to encourage your teen's good behavior. And encouragement is ultimately the best discipline tool ("to teach") we have.

Father: I noticed that you and Damian got home on time last night.

Karen: Yeah, no biggy.

Father: Well, I appreciate you keeping your agreement. It shows responsibility. How are we doing about our half—staying off your back?

Karen: Okay . . . You're showing responsibility.

Father: Good . . . Thanks.

Active Problem–Solving at Home

Choose a problem you would like to handle with your teen using the active problem-solving process. It can be the same one you chose for the logical consequences exercise or a new one that requires more teamwork.

_____

_____

_____

(After you use the process) How did each step go?
1. Identify the problem.

_____

2. Share thoughts and feelings and acknowledge your teen's thoughts and feelings.

_____

3. Generate solutions and guidelines.

_____

4. Decide on logical consequences if needed.

_____

5. Follow up.

_____

What positive results came out of your discussion?

_____

_____

What will you do differently next time to improve the process?

_____

_____

_____

_____

The Problem-Handling Model

Anticipate and prevent problems through Problem-Prevention Talks and Family Talks

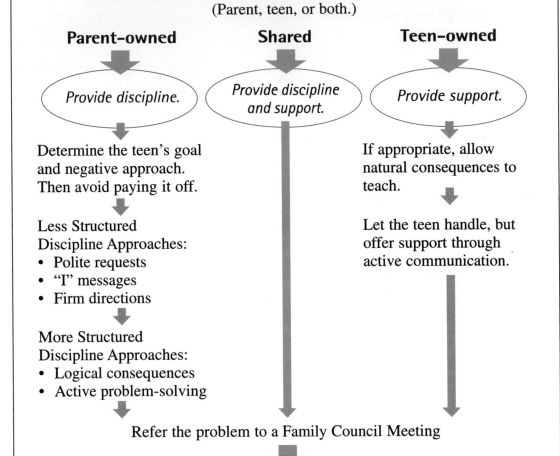

If a problem does occur, determine who owns the problem: (Parent, teen, or both.)

Parent-owned

Provide discipline.

Determine the teen's goal and negative approach. Then avoid paying it off.

Less Structured Discipline Approaches:
- Polite requests
- "I" messages
- Firm directions

More Structured Discipline Approaches:
- Logical consequences
- Active problem-solving

Shared

Provide discipline and support.

Teen-owned

Provide support.

If appropriate, allow natural consequences to teach.

Let the teen handle, but offer support through active communication.

Refer the problem to a Family Council Meeting

And no matter who owns the problem, encourage, encourage, encourage!!!

This model for handling problems includes skills presented in Chapters 2 through 6.
- It begins with preventing many problems through problem-prevention talks (Chapter 3) and family talks (Chapter 6).
- When a problem does occur, determine who owns the problem (Chapter 3).
- If the parent owns the problem or if it is shared, use discipline skills (Chapter 4).

- If the teen owns the problem, or if it is shared, use support skills (Chapter 5).
- In any of the three cases, you may decide to refer the problem to the Family Council Meeting (Chapter 6).
- Of course, encouragement is always necessary (Chapter 2).

Parenting and Anger

Many parents have great difficulty controlling their anger. When parents fly into a rage with their teens, the following results:

- Power struggles increase.
- Their teens want to get revenge.
- Their teens' self-esteem and courage decrease.
- Parents damage their relationship with their children.

This parent's anger is really about fear for her son's safety. She would do better to tell him that.

Many teens, also, are prone to anger. Those who respond to frustration with excessive anger often cause damage to themselves and others and can be painful to live with. Learning to manage anger effectively is crucial for everyone in the family.

Why We Get Angry . . . and Keep Getting Angry

The first step toward controlling anger is to examine why you got angry in the first place. Maybe your teen has hurt you. Maybe you're afraid for her. Maybe your relationship isn't what you'd like it to be. Some parents may have unresolved anger stemming from causes that have nothing to do with their children, such as job stresses, a divorce, or painful, unresolved memories from their own childhood. Sometimes counseling or psychotherapy is needed to heal these wounds.

There are many reasons why anger begins. But people generally *keep* getting angry for the same reason: Their anger gets them positive results; that is, people give them what they want because they got mad. This "pay-off" becomes an incentive to continue losing their temper. Rudolf Dreikurs once said that people don't "lose" their temper, they "use" their temper to bully others into giving in to their demands.

How to Manage Your Anger

1. **Recognize that your anger is a useful message that you send yourself.** Try to determine why you are getting angry.

2. **Evaluate how reasonable your anger is.** Sometimes when we get furious because we don't get our own way, we're being unreasonable. But sometimes our anger is valid—it's telling us that we or our children are in danger.

3. **Think about your options:**

   a. You can ignore your anger and hope the problem goes away. But if it doesn't, you will get angrier. You may even develop physical side effects, such as stomachaches or high blood pressure.

   b. You can change your attitude about what is bothering you. For example, imagine that you are angry because your teenage son has decided not to play football this year. You realize you are angry not because his choice is wrong for *him*, but because he is not living out *your* dreams. Your anger is not reasonable. So you decide to care less about his football career and focus more on his other interests.

Now imagine that you discover your teen has been taking drugs, and you are furious. Give yourself a time-out and think about the situation. Although drug use is a critical issue, you can be thankful that your teen is still alive and healthy. You still have time to be a positive influence.

c. You can use your Active Parenting skills to help solve the problem. The best use of anger is to give us added energy to solve the problem intelligently.

How to Help Your Angry Teen

Show your teen how to deal with his anger by talking with him calmly.

1. **Give him a good model.** *One way your teen will learn how to handle his problems is by watching how you handle yours.*
   - Do you fly into a rage, hurling insults and humiliating people? If you do, then your teen may too.
   - Do you strike out at other people?
   - Do you sulk when you don't get your way?

2. **Tell her how to talk about being mad.**

Examples:

"You have the right to feel the way you do, but in our family we don't scream or blame other people. Let's look for some solutions together."

"I can see that you're angry, But tell me why you're angry instead of hitting things."

"When you get mad at me, please tell me without calling me names. I don't call you names—please don't call me names."

169

3. **Take yourself out of the power struggle.** When your teen has a tantrum, acknowledge his anger but at the same time, "take your sail out of his wind." Instead of fighting with him, step away. By doing so you are telling him that "I am not intimidated by your temper and will not give in, but I won't punish or humiliate you either." Your teen will get neither a fight nor his own way. He will learn that anger is not an effective way to influence people.

4. **Use logical consequences when appropriate.** For example, if your teen's anger leads to the destruction of property, a logical consequence is for him to use his money to pay for the damage. Likewise, if he's disrespectful to you, make yourself available to talk about the problem or his concerns only when he brings himself under control.

Example:

"I can't talk to you when you yell at me. Let me know when you are ready to talk about this respectfully and we'll see if we can work out a solution."

5. **Use active problem-solving to find a solution that works for both of you.** Often, even when the answer is essentially "no," you can negotiate solutions that allow the teen to take away something positive from the discussion. By involving her in the decision-making process, you also make it less necessary for her to rebel in order to get power.

Example:

"I appreciate your agreeing to go with us to the wedding even though you think it's a big waste of time. We'll agree that you can cut out during the reception and watch the basketball game in the hotel room."

Drugs, Sexuality, and Violence: Establish Guidelines

Your teen's ability to make responsible decisions about drugs, sexuality, and violence is critical. The consequences can be life-threatening. The skills presented in this chapter can help you prepare her for the challenges ahead.

Although responsibility applies equally to all three of these areas, I want to focus in this chapter on tobacco, alcohol, and other drugs. We will look at sexuality more closely in Chapter 5 and drugs and violence in Chapter 6.

Ten Prevention Strategies for Parents

Strategy #3. Establish clear guidelines for behavior.

Taking the time to sit with your teen and agree on clear guidelines for behavior can pay off greatly when your teen has to make a choice. It is like taking a test and knowing the correct answers ahead of time. A problem-prevention talk (Chapter 3) is an ideal way to proceed.

Let's review the five steps of the problem-prevention talk:

1. Identify potential problems and risks.
2. Share your thoughts and feelings about these problems and acknowledge your teen's thoughts and feelings.
3. Generate guidelines through brainstorming and negotiation (within limits that you can live with).
4. Decide on logical consequences for violating the guidelines (if necessary).
5. Follow up to ensure that guidelines were followed and to enforce consequences (if necessary).

Some of the areas related to drugs, sexuality, and violence in which you may want to establish guidelines include:

- curfews
- having friends over
- spending nights out
- parties
- when and how to use physical force as defense
- going places that could be dangerous
- dating

Establishing a "No Use" Rule

One of the few formal guidelines for behavior that I recommend is a "no use" rule. Parents and teens together sign an agreement stating that everyone in the family will obey the law as it applies to the use of tobacco, alcohol, and other drugs. It can be stated like this:

"No use of illegal drugs by anyone in the family, and no use of alcohol or nicotine by anyone under the legal age of ___."

Putting the no-use rule in writing and having each family member sign it can add weight to the agreement.

The "no use" rule can be part of your family's discussion about the effects of alcohol and other drugs. All members of the family who are old enough to understand it should sign.

Once the rule is established, it is important for you to let your teen know that you expect her to abide by the rule. This means no experimenting or social use, either. Don't sabotage your own rule by giving the message that "all kids will try it" or that "rules were made to be broken."

Some parents allow their teen to satisfy a curiosity about alcohol or tobacco in a "safe" environment by allowing the teen to sample small amounts at home. While this may be legal in some states, we do not recommend this practice. However, if you choose to go ahead, we strongly urge you to check with the Secretary of State's office first and to make this a one-time event. DO NOT ALLOW REGULAR USE. It is clear that tobacco is a major health hazard at any age, and there is growing evidence that alcohol can interfere with normal teenage development. Of course, marijuana and other illegal substances should not be used by anyone.

For rules to carry impact, they must be backed up by consequences. The use of logical consequences will help enforce the no-use rule. If you have no reason to suspect the use of drugs, I suggest you discuss consequences in general terms only. You might say something like:

"Let's be clear about something. For us to continue to feel good about giving you more freedom and more responsibility, we have to be able to trust you. This no-use rule is largely a matter of trust. We won't be there looking over your shoulder every minute. We won't lock you in your room during your free time. But if you should break that trust, then the responsible thing for us to do is to keep a closer eye on you. That means keeping you home more often, checking up on you more regularly, and otherwise cutting down on your freedom. And since using alcohol or other drugs when driving can be deadly, we would want to protect you and others by not allowing you to use the car."

If your teen has a history of drug or alcohol use or breaks the no-use rule, then the consequences can get more specific. Rather than relying on the common and usually ineffectual consequence of grounding, it is better to use privileges, possessions, and favors that your child wants from you. Remember, it is important that these consequences be logically related to the breaking of the no-use rule. The loss of driving privileges is logically connected to the use of mind-altering substances because they make driving unsafe. Not being allowed to go to parties or concerts for a period of time is logical because trust is needed in these situations, and your teen has temporarily lost your trust. By talking with your teen, your spouse, and other adults, you can come up with a list of consequences that will be meaningful to your teen.

It is important for you to specify how your teen can earn back your trust.

It is important for you to specify how your teen can earn back your trust. If he feels he can never win it back, or that his freedom is gone forever, he may decide to openly rebel and do what he wants to do anyway.

Family Enrichment Activity: Teaching Skills

Most of this chapter has used the word "discipline" to mean setting limits on teen behavior and redirecting negative behavior to positive. But because discipline means to instruct, this chapter's Family Enrichment Activity is to teach your teen something that he

Teaching a skill empowers your teen, helping her become independent.

or she would like to learn. There is a saying that "knowledge is power." A teen who achieves power through a positive approach has less need to rebel. And since you are the one empowering her, it strengthens your relationship.

174

The following tips can help you teach a skill effectively:

1. **Motivate.** Encourage your teen to want to participate by finding a skill he wants to learn. It can be a sport, hobby, or intellectual skill. Increase motivation by making the skill as relevant to his life as possible: "When I teach you how to change the oil yourself, you'll save a lot of money."

2. **Select a good time.** Pick a time when neither of you will be rushed or likely to be interrupted.

3. **Break the skill down into small steps.** This makes it much easier to learn. It also gives the learner many opportunities for success and many chances for the teacher to encourage her to stick with it: "The first step in making the family lasagna recipe is to take out the 9- x 12-inch baking pan and all the ingredients."

4. **Demonstrate.** When teaching a difficult skill, it is helpful to demonstrate the skill yourself (provided you can do it!), explaining slowly as you do: "Let me show you my famous up-and-under move. First you drive to the basket like this. Then you start up like you're going for a lay-up, like this. Then, when the bigger player goes to block your shot, you pull the ball down and swing it under his arms for an underhanded lay-up, like this. Well . . . you get the idea."

5. **Let your teen try.** Let him perform the skill while you stand by, ready to offer help if needed. Be gentle about mistakes, and keep a sense of humor: "Okay, now you try. Just remember to take it slow and easy, and if you see a flashing blue light, pull over."

6. **Encourage, encourage, encourage.** Make plenty of encouraging comments that acknowledge your teen's efforts as well as results: "Great! That's the way to do it!"

7. **Work or play together.** Once your teen has learned the skill to an appropriate level, work or play together so that you can both enjoy the companionship of the activity: "Okay, Tiger, let's go play a round of golf."

Teaching Skills

Remember When . . .

Think about a skill that one of your parents taught you. Close your eyes for a moment and visualize the experience.

What was the activity?_____

How did you feel about your parent at that moment?_____

How did you feel about yourself?_____

What mistakes did your parents make that you could avoid?_____

What positive things did your parent do that you could do too?_____

Now You Try

Pick an activity you would like to work on with your teen, such as:

- a sport skill
- something to do with the car
- cooking a special dish
- opening a bank account
- saying "no" to someone and without looking like a jerk

Talk it over with your teen first, then list here the skills you will teach.

Teen's Name	Skill to Be Taught
_____	_____
_____	_____
_____	_____

Use these six steps as a checklist after you've taught the skill:

1. Did you motivate your teen to want to learn?
2. Did you select a good time when you weren't rushed?
3. Did you first demonstrate the skill?
4. Did you let your teen try?
5. Did you work alongside your teen?
6. Did you acknowledge her efforts?

What went well?_____

What might you do better next time?_____

_____

_____

_____

Chapter **4** | *Home Activities*

Now take a break and put some of these new skills to use.

1. Re-read any part of Chapter 4 that you'd like.
2. Use the following skills to handle a problem with your teen. (Fill in the guide sheets on pages 146 and 147: Polite requests, "I" messages, Firm directions.)
3. Have an active problem-solving discussion with your teen to come up with a logical consequence for a problem behavior you are experiencing. (Fill in the guide sheet on pages 157 and 158.)
4. Teach your teen something you're both interested in.

Cooperation
and Communication

Chapter 5

Communication Case Studies

Lizzie, fifteen, had the physical maturity of a grown woman and the emotions of a teenager. She really liked twenty-one-year-old Grant. He was good-looking, confident, and grown-up—not like the boys at her school, who were just kids. Her mom, knowing that beautiful Lizzie looked much older than her fifteen years, was worried. She repeatedly warned Lizzie about getting involved with older guys, but Lizzie dismissed her "nagging." She could handle it, she said to herself. She was really mature. Besides, Grant really liked her. In reality Grant wasn't interested in having a fifteen-year-old girlfriend. He figured she would be easy, though, and he wanted a good time. It didn't take much to persuade her to have sex. Afterwards, Lizzie was happy, thinking the physical intimacy meant Grant was committed to her. Little did she know then that he wouldn't even be around when the pregnancy test turned out positive. Now she had to tell her mother. It was going to be the hardest thing she'd ever done.

Raymond, twelve, told himself this wasn't the end of the world, that lots of kids went through it these days. But when his dad had told him he was moving out, it was like the air had been kicked out of him. How could his parents be getting a divorce? Sure, they fought a lot, but they had always assured him that their fighting was no big deal. Now he'd be lucky to see his dad every two weeks. Suddenly, Raymond hated everything about his life.

Samantha, seventeen, was devastated. Being overweight had always bothered her, but she had managed to live with it. She had friends, and she was good in school. But nothing this bad had ever happened to her before. How could guys be so cruel? Samantha recalled the scene with shame. She had been walking through the parking lot of the mall with her friends drinking a slurpee, when a carload of guys drove by. One of them leaned out of the window and yelled at Samantha: "Get your fat *** on a diet." As he drew his head in, everyone in the car roared with laughter. Her friends told Samantha not to let it bother her. "That guy's a jerk," they reassured her. But now she lay on her bed, staring at the ceiling and wondering what other people said about her behind her back.

A loving and supportive parent can help a troubled teen learn and grow from the pain.

Being a teenager is often painful. No one gets through it without some suffering. During hard times, we can reach out to our teens to provide support. We can comfort, encourage, and help them use their problems to grow stronger. *Our role in such situations is not to discipline.* Lizzie does not need a lecture on birth control at this moment, nor does she need to be grounded—both common parental tactics in this situation. She needs first and foremost the love and support of a caring parent. Raymond doesn't need his dad to tell him to buck up and face it like a man; he needs a dad who is sympathetic and understands the pain his son is experiencing. And Samantha doesn't need a parent saying "I told you so" about her weight. Right now, she needs to know that she is loved and accepted as is. She needs an ally to help her face the cruelties of the world.

Supporting our teens when they hit a storm can mean the difference between stability and growth and a failure cycle. Such situations also present opportunities to teach the value of cooperation as we help our children explore options for handling their problems. Cooperation, along with courage, responsibility, and self-esteem, is one of the four essential qualities that help our teens thrive in our society. We define it as follows:

Cooperation: Two or more people working together in a mutually supportive manner toward a common goal.

The teen who learns to work cooperatively with others in solving problems has a far greater chance of success. That's why we will look at the skills you can use to help support your teen in solving her own problems. These skills include:

- Natural consequences (Chapter 4)
- Active communication (this chapter)
- Family council meetings (Chapter 6)

Communication

Communication with teens is not easy. It requires patience and skill. Why does it often seem so hard?

- Teens' self-esteem is fragile, so they're quick to interpret what you say as disrespectful.
- Because teens are trying to become independent adults, they often identify with their friends and not with you. Often they would rather communicate with a friend than a parent.
- Teens are busy experimenting with who they are in ways that you may not approve of, from clothing choices to hair color to nose rings. Arguments with your teen about such experimentation can keep you from communicating about deeper issues.

- Many teens feel that no one listens to them or cares what they think. They don't *expect* to be able to communicate with you.
- Teens are at a stage of life when they are confused about who they are and what they think. Sometimes they just don't *know* what to say—they may not even know what they think.

Despite these issues, many teens (according to one study, about forty percent of them) wish their parents spent more time with them. Under all the funny hair and aloof attitude, this alien person is still your child, and she still wants your support and acceptance. She may be pushing you away most of the time, but deep down she needs to hear from you more often.

Mixed Messages

Communicating with your teen involves a lot more than what you say. You also get your message across through your tone of voice and through your body language—what you do with your hands, whether you stand near or far from someone, your facial expressions, etc. Your teen actually "hears" these two communication methods more than your words. Studies have shown that people pay most attention to body language, then tone of voice, and lastly what is said. *Often how you say something is even more important than what you say.*

Often how you say something is even more important than what you say.

One surefire way to miscommunicate with your teen is to say one thing with your words and something different with your tone and body language. Mixed messages cause a lot of problems.

Imagine that your teen owns a problem and you have decided to let her handle it. You say: "I'm not angry. You can do whatever you like." But your face and tone say: "I'll be very angry if you don't do what I think is best." This sort of mixed signal makes it difficult for your teen to know where she really stands with you. You may need to adjust your attitude so that you really accept her right to make the decision without feeling anger. You may still be somewhat disappointed if she makes a particular choice, but you can change your words to be more consistent.

Example:

"I may be disappointed if you decide not to take your sister with you to the mall, but as I said, it's your choice. I can live with it." Your face and tone need to say this, too.

If you give a mixed message while disciplining your teen, you are giving your teen an "out," because she'll probably listen only to the part of the message she wants to hear. It is much more powerful to give just one clear message.

For example, suppose your teen asks you if he can go to a concert on a school night. Your words say one thing: "I don't think that's a very good idea." But your tone says something different: "I'm not really that concerned. If you go ahead, that's your business. I don't care."

What do you think your teen will do? Since more of the message is carried through tone of voice, he's probably going to go to the concert. He might not even realize you don't want him to go. An important principle of communication is this: The clearer you are, the stronger your message is. So deliver the same message with your tone of voice and body language as you're conveying with your words.

Avoiding Communication Blocks

If your teen pays you the great compliment of sharing a problem with you, she is putting her self-esteem at risk. Will you be judgmental? Will you blame her or criticize? If you say or do anything at this point to injure her self-esteem, she will withdraw. You will have blocked communication.

**A communication block is any remark or attitude
on the part of the speaker that injures the listener's self-esteem
and shuts down communication.**

*Many parents think they're helping their teens by placating
or offering advice. This isn't supporting the teen; it's
blocking communication.*

Because you communicate your attitude largely through tone of voice and body language, it is not enough just to watch your words. You have to adopt a supportive, nonjudgmental attitude if you are really going to help. When you listen with an attitude of support, your teen will begin to trust you with her feelings and share more of what is going on in her life. This sets the stage for you to influence her to make wise decisions. If you jump the gun and block communication, you will have lost this valuable opportunity to offer guidance and win cooperation.

Look at the list of common communication blocks on page 185. Each block ignores the teen's own thoughts and feelings and instead focuses on the parent's attempt to control the situation. More often than not, these attempts backfire. When people are in pain, they want to know that someone else feels their pain with them. The mistake parents make is launching into an attempt to solve the teen's problem instead of offering any sympathy or encouragement. Ironically, if you try to solve your teen's problems, you will actually diminish her self-esteem. *Your goal is not to take over and provide a solution, or to take away your teen's pain.* It is to offer a caring ear, support, and encouragement, and to help your teen find a useful solution for herself.

Your goal is not to take over and provide a solution, or to take away your teen's pain.

The first step in helping is to identify your most common pitfalls. Once you are aware that you use them, be on guard the next time your teen has a problem, and avoid these pitfalls. When you find yourself using them in the future, catch yourself with a smile and make a change.

Communication Blocks

Block:	Example:	Parent's Intention:	What It Really Says to the Teen:
Commanding	"What you should do is . . ." "Stop complaining."	To control the situation and provide quick solutions.	"You don't have the right to decide how to handle your own problems."
Giving Advice	"I've got a really good idea . . ." "Why don't you . . ."	To solve the problem for the teen	"You don't have the good sense to come up with your own solutions."
Placating	"It isn't as bad as it seems." "Everything will be okay."	To take away the teen's pain; to make her feel better.	You don't have a right to your feelings. You can't handle discomfort."
Interrogating	"What did you do to make him . . ."	To get to the bottom of the problem and find out what the teen did wrong	"You must have messed up somewhere."
Distracting	"Let's not worry about that." "Let's . . ."	To protect the teen from the problem by changing the subject	"I don't think you can stand the discomfort long enough to find a real solution."
Psychologizing	"Do you know why you said that?" "You're just being oversensitive."	To help prevent future problems by analyzing the teen's behavior and explaining his motives	"I know more about you than you know about yourself. Therefore, I'm superior to you."
Sarcasm	"Well, I guess that's just about the end of the world."	To show the teen how wrong her attitudes or behavior are by making her feel ridiculous	"You are ridiculous."
Moralizing	"The right thing to do would be to . . ." "You really should . . ."	To show the teen the proper way to deal with the problem	"I'll choose your values for you."
Know-It-All	"You know what you should do?" "I'll tell you."	To show the teen that he has a resource for handling any problem—you.	"Since I know it all, you must know nothing."

Active Communication

Active listening means listening with your eyes as well as your ears to what your teen is communicating—not just the words, but also what she is feeling.

Instead of blocking communication, you can use "active communication," a set of skills that will help you win cooperation and support your teen in solving problems. Active communication is recommended when your teen owns a problem you'd like to help her solve, or when you both share responsibility for a problem. There are five steps:

1. Listen actively.
2. Listen for feelings.
3. Connect feelings to content.
4. Look for alternatives and evaluate consequences.
5. Follow up later.

① Listen actively.

What do I mean by "active" listening? If you listen fully, you don't just receive information; you are an active participant in the communication process. You listen with your eyes as well as your ears, with your intuition as well as your thinking. With active listening, you're trying to encourage your teen to express what he is thinking and feeling. Here's how:

- **Give full attention.** Your teen may feel encouraged by the attention alone. It says, "I care about you. You matter. I'm here to help."

- **Keep your own talk to a minimum.** When your mouth is open, your ears don't work as well. So listen, and don't talk.

- **Acknowledge what you are hearing.** Let your teen know that you are understanding, that you are taking her words to heart. You can say something as simple as "I see" now and then or even "Uh-huh." Ask questions to clarify what your teen is saying or to summarize long stories.

- **Listen with empathy.** Empathy means sharing another person's feelings. Allow yourself to feel some of what your teen is feeling, and show her with your tone of voice and facial expressions that you feel what she is saying. In short, listen to the feelings beneath your teen's words.

Examples:

"Lizzie, you look like you just lost your best friend. What happened?"

"Raymond, I know this is hard for you. Let's talk."

"Oh, Samantha . . . that must have really hurt."

(2.) Listen for feelings.

Your teen needs to acknowledge and accept his feelings rather than keep them bottled up. Some teens keep their feelings so repressed that they eventually act out violently or suffer from stress-related sicknesses such as stomachaches or headaches. Teach him to say how he feels and then to reflect on his feelings before he decides what action to take.

You can do this by listening for your teen's feelings, not just the content of the story. Until a teen has been taught to describe his feelings with words, you will have to listen closely to his tone of voice and watch his face to discover what he is feeling. By listening this way, you communicate the most powerful message of all: You care.

"This is a really scary situation for you, Lizzie, isn't it?"

"You have a right to be angry at me, Raymond. I let you down."

"You're worried about what the other kids really think about your weight, aren't you?"

(3.) Connect feelings to content.

When you have actively listened to what your teen has to say and have an idea of what he is feeling, the next step is to reflect those feelings back to him. You can become what psychologist Haim Ginott calls an "emotional mirror." Mirrors don't judge how we look or tell us what to do. They just reflect what is there. Reflect your teen's feelings and then connect them to what happened—the "content."

"You sound really concerned about what you're going to do about the baby, Lizzie."

"I guess you're worried about what's going to go wrong next, Raymond."

"Samantha, you seem angry at them for being so cruel."

By reflecting feelings in tentative terms ("It sounds as though . . .";
"I guess . . .") you don't sound like you're trying to be a

188

mind-reader or a know-it-all. If you miss your guess about what your teen is feeling, she can correct you. That way you're sure you understand what she is saying and feeling.

Example:

Lizzie: "No . . . it's not that. I want to have the baby. I just can't believe he didn't care anything for me."

Mother: "I see. You're really surprised he ran out that way."

By adjusting to the teen's correction, the communication continues to flow.

When you do reflect the feeling accurately, an exciting thing will happen. Your teen will nod her head in recognition, maybe say "yes," and then continue to share. She will feel understood and cared for—and she may understand herself a little better.

Connecting Feelings to Content

What the Teen Says:	Feeling Word	What the Parent Says:
"Mom, I'm not going to do John's dishes again!"	Angry	"You seem angry that I want you to clean all the dishes."
"I missed the foul shot, and we lost the game."	Disappointed	"Sounds like you're disappointed about missing the shot."
"I hate the way I look in this uniform."	Embarrassed	"I guess you're embarrassed to wear that hat."

4. Look for alternatives and evaluate consequences.

Once you have established a level of empathy, you can begin to encourage your teen to look at possible solutions.

Examples:

"What can you do about that?"

"What else can you try?"

After each alternative, help your teen predict the consequences of that alternative.

Example:

"What do you think would happen if you did that?"

It is better for your teen to think of alternatives on her own, without prompting. This keeps her from getting angry at you and allows her to take full credit for the solution. If she cannot think of any alternatives, you can tentatively suggest some. You can also share a personal experience in a similar situation, such as:

"I don't know what you will decide to do, Samantha. I remember one time when I was in high school and some of the boys teased me about being . . . well . . . not very busty. I felt humiliated and sad, then angry at them for being cruel and stupid."

Try not to tell your teen what to do. She must choose if she is to learn responsibility.

Try not to tell your teen what to do. She must choose if she is to learn responsibility. When she decides what to do, she feels higher self-esteem and accepts responsibility for her choices.

Your position during this discussion should be what we call "palms up." A palms-up gesture says to your teen, "I don't know what you will decide to do. The decision is in your hands." By actually turning your palms up while saying, "I don't know what you will decide to do," you communicate that you are a supportive, non-threatening ally. Contrast this with the finger-pointing position of the dictator who says, "Here's what you need to do," and you can see how the palms-up approach actually increases your ability to influence your teen's decisions. After all, why shouldn't he listen to your alternatives? You're out to empower him, not control him.

5. Follow up later.

Before ending the discussion, ask your teen what he intends to do, and when. Do this gently. Even Einstein needed time to think about new information before he knew what step was next.

After your teen has had an opportunity to handle the problem, follow up by asking how the solution turned out.

Example:

"How did it go with..."

Following up later to see how your teen handled a difficult situation shows your teen that you really care about her.

By following up, you will not only help your teen make sense of the experience, but you will also confirm to him that your interest is genuine. If the problem still exists, you can also start active communication over again to find another solution.

Putting Active Communication to Work

Now that you are aware of the five steps of the active communication process, look for opportunities to use them to help your teen solve her own problems. You'll find that the more supportive you are, the more cooperative your teen is likely to be.

If you find you are still fighting with your teen a lot, however, he may not be willing yet to sit down for a long discussion. You can still listen for his feelings and express your empathy.

Examples:

"Boy, you sure look down."

"I guess you're really ticked off."

"That must have hurt."

You can even use this skill when disciplining your teen or telling him he can't do something. It may help reduce his anger. Just having his feelings recognized and accepted can sometimes help.

Examples:

"I know you're angry that I won't let you go."

"I'm sorry my decision feels so bad to you."

"If looks could kill, I'd be in real trouble right now."

"I can live with you not liking me very much right now, but I don't think I could live with myself if something terrible happened to you."

Feeling Words

Although the English language has hundreds of words that describe specific feelings, most people do not use many in their daily vocabulary. As you practice looking for the right "feeling words," you will find your feeling word vocabulary increases and the job gets easier. To help with this process, we have included a list of feeling words for you to keep in mind.

Words that describe pleasant feelings

accepted	hopeful		
adequate	honored		
adventurous	important		
bold	joyful		
brilliant	lovely		
calm	loving		
caring	overjoyed		
cheerful	peaceful		
comfortable	peppy		
confident	playful		
content	pleased		
daring	proud		
eager	refreshed		
elated	relieved		
encouraged	satisfied		
energetic	secure		
fascinated	successful		
free	surprised		
full	sympathetic		
glad	tranquil		
great	understood		
gutsy	warm		
happy	wonderful		
high	zany		

Words that describe unpleasant feelings

afraid	jealous
angry	let down
anxious	lonely
ashamed	miserable
bashful	nervous
bored	overwhelmed
cautious	pained
cheated	possessive
concerned	provoked
defeated	pushed
defiant	rejected
disappointed	remorseful
discouraged	resentful
down	shy
embarrassed	stupid
envious	suspicious
frustrated	trapped
guilty	uncomfortable
hateful	uneasy
hesitant	unhappy
hopeless	unloved
hurt	unsure
impatient	weary
irritated	worried

Connecting Feelings to Content Practice

The following scene from the *Active Parenting of Teens* video offers a good example of the entire active communication process in action. See if you can identify where the five steps are used. Try to:

- circle the feeling words
- underline where you see a connection between feelings to content
- bracket the alternatives and consequence.

Mother: Hey. You seem pretty miserable. You've never skipped school before.

Jarret: Well, I'm not going so don't even try.

Mother: You sound pretty angry about it.

Jarret: You would be too.

Mother: I see. What's happened to get you so upset?

Jarret: Nothing.

Mother: Sometimes it helps to talk about it.

Jarret: I doubt it . . . and it's not going to make me change my mind about going.

Mother: Well, I can't make you go, Jarret. And I don't know what you're going to decide to do, but I would like to talk to you about it.

Jarret: Well, Steve, he's a senior and the editor of the yearbook and I'm on the staff for the ninth grade and he called this big meeting and started yelling about people missing deadlines and stuff and the only person he called out by name was me.

Mother: Oh Jarret, that must have really hurt.

Jarret: I wanted to crawl under a desk and die.

Mother: Pretty embarrassing!

Jarret: Exactly. I've never been so humiliated. I just can't go back there!

Mother: I can see why you'd feel that way.

Jarret: You can?

Mother: I can remember . . . well, maybe I shouldn't tell you this.

Jarret: Come on! I told you . . .

Mother: Well, okay . . . . See, I was already a senior, and I went to the movies with a date and we parked. All we did was kiss a little, but he told everyone I was really easy and implied we'd done a lot more . . .

Jarret: What a jerk.

Mother: I called him worse, believe me, but it was incredibly embarrassing—what happened.

Jarret: Well, what can I do? I can't call him a jerk. Besides, I *have* missed some deadlines.

Mother: I see. So as your editor he expects you to handle your responsibilities.

Jarret: I guess . . . But he didn't have to yell at me in front of everyone!

Mother: No, I agree. That was uncalled for. Well, let's look at your options. You can hang out here with me the rest of your life.

Connecting Feelings to Content Practice *continued*

Jarret: Ugh. No offense.

Mother: None taken. Okay, so what else could you do?

Jarret: I could just quit the yearbook. Write him a note or something.

Mother: You could quit. How would that make you feel?

Jarret: Like a quitter.

Mother: Doesn't sound like you, anyway. Tell me something—is this Steve guy really a bad guy or was he maybe just feeling the pressures himself?

Jarret: Both. He's yelled at other people before.

Mother: I see. Well, you know, there's something you need to know about the world of work. Some bosses are like that, and you have to decide whether you want to work with them or go someplace else. Of course, when you miss deadlines, you get fired, too.

Jarret: Yeah, it's not that bad. I mean, he does compliment me on my work, sometimes.

Mother: What if you asked to talk to him and told him how you felt about what happened?

Jarret: Well ....

Mother: I know. It would take a lot of courage.

Jarret: Well, I'll think about it.

Mother: Let me know how it goes, okay?

Answers are on page 240.

Active Communication Practice

Practice active communication at home whenever you can. Afterwards, complete these questions so you can learn from the experience.

What was the situation or problem you talked to your teen about?

_____

_____

How did you approach your teen?

_____

_____

List examples of the five steps of active communication that you were able to use:

1) Listen actively_____

2) Listen for feelings _____

3) Connect feelings to content _____

4) Look for alternatives and evaluate consequences _____

5) Follow up later _____

How did you teen respond to your effort?

_____

_____

What did you like about how you handled the process?

_____

_____

What would you do differently next time?

_____

_____

_____

_____

Drugs, Sexuality, and Violence: Talking about Sexual Behavior and Values

I explained earlier that the purpose of these sections was not to tell you what values are right for you and your children, but rather to help you develop the skills for communicating those values to them. In this section, we will focus mainly on values associated with sexuality as we explore how to communicate your values to your teens.

What do you want for your teen?

Before you can communicate your values to your teens, you need to first clarify what you yourself believe. If you are married, talk this over with your spouse. You may find that you don't agree on everything. That's okay, because your teen won't agree with either of you 100 percent anyway. Remember, your job is to influence, not control. You can't force your values on your teen.

Frequent discussions about values with your teen is more effective than one long talk.

Some questions you may want to think about:

- What is the purpose of sex? Is it just to procreate? Is it also a means of expressing love? Is it meant to give pleasure?

- Is it okay to enjoy sex without love? Without marriage?

- What do you believe about fidelity? Is extramarital sex wrong?

- Do you believe in birth control?

- Do you believe in a woman's right to choose abortion?

- What responsibility does a person have for his sexual partner?

- What's the difference between seduction and date rape?

- What do you believe about homosexuality? If you found out that your teen was gay, would you still be a loving parent?

- Is masturbation an acceptable way to release sexual tension? If so, how much is too much? If not, why? Is there an alternative?

Once you have clarified your own values, you will be in a more powerful position to influence your teen.

Notes:_____

_____

_____

_____

_____

_____

_____

_____

Skills for Talking about Your Values

- **Show respect.** Your teen is entitled to his own opinions and should not be put down for believing something you don't. Keep the lines of communication open.

- **Avoid communication blocks.** You will not only end the conversation, you'll also motivate her to rebel against your values. If you command your teen to believe something, then the only way for her to feel as if she has power over herself is to believe the opposite!

- **Listen for her feelings and consider her thoughts.** Your teen's feelings change rapidly during these years. She may not know why she holds certain values. Help her to decide for herself by listening closely and repeating what you hear.

Examples:

"It sounds like you felt embarrassed when all the guys were talking about how far they got with their dates."

"I guess you're saying you think Dad and I make too big a deal out of sex—that you believe it's just something two people can do together to have a good time."

- **Encourage your teen when he expresses a value you approve of.** For example, if you would like your teenage son to learn to treat women respectfully, catch him being respectful and make a positive comment.

Example:

"I couldn't help overhearing you talking with Mike in the kitchen tonight. I heard you say you didn't think referring to a girl in the 10th grade as 'an easy piece' was a cool thing to say. I just wanted to tell you that I agree with you, and I'm proud of you."

- **Set a positive example.** As with anything, what you do is more important than what you say. If what you say is at odds with what your children see you doing, then your credibility is lost. You won't be able to influence them. Remember, your teen won't follow your lead if he doesn't respect you. Without that respect, your teen will not care what you think or do.

- **Take time to talk about values and beliefs concerning sex, not just the facts.** Keep in mind that your teen really needs to trust you before he'll confide in you about so personal a subject. Earn his trust by respecting his opinions, even if you disagree, and not judging or speaking to him harshly if he opens up.

By staying low-key and nonjudgmental, you may one day find that you have been more of an influence than you thought at the time.

Remember that teens often try values the way they do styles of clothes. Both change often. Both are sometimes tried on for shock value. Both are usually outgrown. *By staying low-key and nonjudgmental, you may one day find that you have been more of an influence than you thought at the time.*

What happens if your beliefs differ dramatically from your teen's? Must you remain silent? Not at all! Instead, you can disagree with your teen respectfully, and calmly state your own opinion. This works best with palms up and an "I don't know what you'll decide" attitude.

Example:

"I respect your right to think of sex as just another way for people to enjoy each other. My own opinion, however, is that sex can be something very special, if it's saved for a special time with a special person. I'm sure that casual sex can be fun, but I think you pay a price for treating it cheaply. You may never know how really great it can be when it's used only as an expression of love and commitment."

The soft-sell approach used in the above example will give the teen something to think about. His dad has not forced a confrontation; the door is left open for the teen to accept later this parent's view as his own. Dad's tone is caring rather than judgmental, and he has appealed to his son's sense of reason rather than using his authoritative position to command agreement.

Once you begin looking, you will find many opportunities to begin a discussion about sexual values. Use TV shows, movies, and news items as openers for these discussions. In these instances, find something in the story that has to do with sexuality and turn it into a question.

Example:

"I saw something on a TV movie last night that I wanted your opinion on. This guy and girl meet in a bar and get pretty drunk. They go home together and have sex, but they are either too drunk or just don't care because they don't use birth control. She gets pregnant. He says it's not his fault because he was drunk, and besides, it's the woman's job to take care of protection. What do you think?"

When you talk about values:

- show respect
- avoid communication blocks
- listen to thoughts and feelings
- come from caring, not judgment
- come from reason, not authority

Ten Prevention Strategies for Parents

Strategy #4. Provide healthy opportunities for challenge.

When I was seventeen, I had the opportunity to experience an "Outward Bound" course in the Blue Ridge Mountains for a month. Every morning at daybreak we were roused from our sleep and ran three miles, to an ice-cold dip in a mountain stream. The day only got harder: We ran, hiked, climbed, and otherwise pitted ourselves against the elements. It was the most demanding physical experience of my life, but when it was over, I felt that I had moved from childhood to adulthood.

Many teens do not get enough opportunities to truly challenge themselves in positive ways. For too many teens, life is boring. Many resort to challenging themselves in dangerous ways just to feel a rush of adrenaline.

How can parents help? First, work with community leaders to make outdoor programs available to all teens in your community. In the meantime, help your own teen to take advantage of activities that are currently available. Look into hiking, rock-climbing, or cycling clubs; white-water sports; scouting programs; and programs such as Outward Bound. Organized sports offer excellent opportunities to challenge in positive ways. School leagues, recreation department leagues, and youth groups such as the YMCA and the Boys Club offer plenty of opportunities for girls and boys to get physical in healthy ways.

In addition to physical challenges, you can also encourage your teens to pursue hobbies and other interests in which they challenge themselves to develop skills and knowledge. Possibilities include chess clubs, working on the school newspaper, skill-building jobs, junior business clubs, community service work, and playing a musical instrument. If your teen can find an interest that challenges her to stick with it and do her best, her confidence will grow and she will satisfy her desire for excitement in positive ways.

Ten Prevention Strategies for Parents

Strategy #5. Consult with teens about how to resist peer pressure.

Most people realize that to "just say no" to drugs, sexual activity, or violence is a lot easier said than done. Have you never knuckled under to people around you and eaten something off of your diet, or bought something you really didn't want? The pressures on teens, with their strong desire to belong, is a lot greater.

Peer pressure is more subtle and strong than most people realize.

Helping your teen come up with strong comeback lines to peer pressure can help her build the confidence to stand up for what she believes.

Imagine that four teens are sitting around talking, and one lights up a marijuana joint. Two of the others say "great" and take a hit. The third hands it to your teen, expecting that she'll want to smoke some, too. Let's say she doesn't want to, but she doesn't want to look foolish or childish either. She feels the pressure to do what they're doing without anyone actually telling her to follow along. What's she going to do? Say "no"? Go along anyway? Take a puff, but not inhale? You can increase the chances of her saying "no" by coaching her ahead of time about how to handle such difficult situations.

Resisting peer pressure requires three main things:

1. Knowing your rights

2. The courage to do what's right

3. A good comeback line.

1. Knowing Your Rights

Help your teen realize that she has the right to say "no" to peer pressure. Her goals and values for her life are important. She needs to know this. Also, encourage her by accepting that she may not always agree with you any more than she does her friends. You may feel frustrated when she argues with you, but she'll need that strong will to stand up to her peers when they want her to cave in.

2. The Courage to Do What's Right

Help your teen recognize that he is strong enough to do what's right by pointing out his strength each time he exhibits it.

Examples:

"I really appreciate you going to the wedding with us even though it meant missing the game on TV."

"I'm proud of the way you told us the truth about the party this weekend, even though you knew we wouldn't let you go since it isn't supervised."

3. A Good Comeback Line

Because teens are desperate to save face in all circumstances, they need to be able to say "no" in a way that doesn't leave them feeling foolish. Going over potential peer pressure situations before they happen and helping your teen prepare comeback lines can be a huge help.

SITUATION #1:

"What's the matter, you're too chicken to fight?"

What you could say to your teen about violence or fighting:

_____

_____

A good comeback line you could offer:

_____

_____

Here's a sample conversation:

Father: Okay, here's the situation. You pull into a parking lot just as another car is pulling in. You get the parking place, but the other guy gets out of the car and is really mad. You two start exchanging words, and you can see that he wants to fight. What do you do?

Son: That's a hard one.

Father: You're right. It is.

Son: I'd tell him that we better cool down before the cops throw us both in jail.

Father: Hey, that's pretty quick. Any other ideas?

SITUATION #2:

"Here, take a hit off this joint."

What you could say to your teen about drugs:

_____

_____

A good comeback line you could offer:

_____

_____

Here's a sample conversation:

Father: So what could you say if you were at a party and three guys just took a hit of marijuana and offered you a smoke?

Daughter: No thanks?

Father: Well, that would work. But what if they pushed harder?

Daughter: I don't know.

Father: Well, how about, "Are you crazy?! My parents will find out and I'll have to wait till I move out before I'm allowed to go to another party."

Daughter: That's good. Or I could say, "You guys are idiots for putting that stuff in your body."

Father: That would take a lot of courage. But it may make them think twice about what they're doing.

Come on, everybody's having sex these days!"

What you could say to your teen about sex:

_____

_____

A good comeback line you could offer:

_____

_____

Here's a sample conversation:

Mother: What would you say if a girl got you alone and started undressing you?

Son: Thank you, God?

Mother: That's not exactly the answer I was hoping for.

Son: I'm kidding. That's not going to happen.

Mother: Don't be so sure. I read this true story in a magazine. A girl had been drinking and went into a boy's dorm room—they were in college. She came on to him and he slept with her. The next week she claimed rape, saying she was too drunk to know what she was doing. He didn't get convicted of rape, but he wound up having to leave school because everybody thought it was his fault.

Son: Wow. That's not fair.

Mother: Right. What would you do if it happened to you?

Son: I guess I'd tell her I'd better take her home so she can get some sleep.

Mother: That would take some willpower, but it's the right thing to do.

Family Enrichment Activity: Expressing Love

Building a positive relationship with teens is an ongoing process, and it takes steady effort. It includes having fun together, teaching specific skills, and showing them respect. Most of all, a positive relationship between parent and teen needs love. All teens need to know that whatever else may happen, their parents love them.

Your teen is never too old to hear the words "I love you!"

You can show your teen you love him in many small ways: a kiss, a pat on the back, tousling his hair, putting your arm around his shoulder. But you also need to *tell* him that you love him. The words may be awkward if you're not used to saying them. But they're beautiful to your teen, even if he rolls his eyes in embarrassment.

Your assignment is to find ways to express your love to your teens, including actually saying "I love you."

Expressing Love

Remember When . . .

Recall a time when an adult in your life expressed love to you. Maybe it was a parent, a grandparent, another relative, or a teacher. Maybe the expression was through words, maybe through an action like a pat on the back.

Describe the experience:

_____

_____

_____

_____

How did you feel?

_____

_____

_____

_____

Expressing Love at Home

To help you remember to tell your teen you love her, fill in the following chart:

Teen's Name	Your Expression	Your Teen's Response

Chapter 5 | *Home Activities*

1. Re-read any of Chapter 5 that you want to review.
2. Practice active communication with your teen, and complete the activity sheet on page 197.
3. Tell your teen you love him, and complete the activity sheet on page 210.

The Problem–Solving Family in Action

Chapter 6

Problems as Opportunities

Problems take time, they generate unpleasant feelings, and they often bring negative consequences. But *they also present opportunities for learning and growth.*

To turn problems into learning experiences, your family members—including your teen—must participate in problem-solving. All the skills we have been learning throughout this book are designed to help you bring your teen into the problem-solving process, from problem-prevention talks to discipline skills (such as active problem-solving and logical consequences) to support skills (such as active communication). Involving your teen in family problem-solving reduces power struggles and increases your influence in your teen's life.

This chapter will present two additional parenting skills for accomplishing these goals:

Family talks are brief discussions on important family topics. They provide an opportunity to:
- discuss values and attitudes in an environment that's nonconfrontational.
- influence your teen's future behavior
- help build your teen's character.

Family council meetings, more structured than family talks, are weekly meetings in which all members of the family have a voice in making family decisions. They may involve problem-solving, family talks, and other skills presented in this book.

Family Talks

Family talks focus on specific topics of interest or importance to family members, such as honesty, depression, television viewing, family roots, career choices, race relations, equality, advertising, and, of course, drugs, sexuality, and violence. It is up to you and your family to determine what topic you will discuss each week.

Teenagers take in information about the world from all of their experiences—what happens at school, what they see on TV, what happens in friends' homes. If parents don't make a special effort to be one of these influences, their teens will learn about the world without them. Take the time to sit down with your family and talk about issues that you'd truly like to hear their opinions on. Share your own opinions. Your time will be well spent. Family talks provide you with the opportunity to discuss your values with your teen on a regular basis. Although values cannot be dictated, you *can* teach values by providing information and sound reasoning, as long as you always demonstrate these values through your actions.

The following tips will help you set up successful family talks.

1. Plan how you will introduce the topic.

This step applies to the first talk only, since family members will pick the topics together from then on.

Example:

"The topic I'd like to introduce for this week's family talk is 'honesty.' Why is a person's word so valuable?"

2. Think of questions that will stimulate discussion.

Ask some questions to keep the discussion moving.

Example:

- Why do you think it's important to be honest?
- How is keeping our agreements a form of honesty?
- How do you feel when someone has lied to you or has not kept an agreement?
- How can we change agreements if we need to?

3. Write down key points you want to make before having your family talk.

Being prepared with key points you wish to make helps keep your family talk informative and on track.

- The more people trust you, the more they can accept your word without having to check up on you.
- It is easier to keep someone's trust than to win it back once you have lost it.
- The more we trust you, the more freedom we can give you.
- Let's all agree to work hard at keeping our agreements and telling the truth.

Influencing our teen's values requires accurate information and sound reasoning. With topics such as drugs, sexuality, or violence you may want to do some research on your own to update your knowledge.

4. Find support materials to help provide information or stimulate discussion.

Look for videos, audiocassettes, excerpts from books, and magazine articles. Watching certain television shows together can be a starting place for a family talk. Keep your eyes open, and you'll find many such resources for making your talks more interesting and informative.

5. Establish ground rules for your talks.

Using good communication skills can mean the difference between a positive family talk and a frustrating experience for everyone. Get agreement from the entire family on ground rules to help everyone communicate effectively. Use the following tips as a starting place.

Communication Tips

DO
- speak respectfully.
- invite everyone's ideas.
- share how you think and feel.
- ask yourself how others feel (in order to see issues from their points of view).
- compliment others.

DON'T
- put anyone's ideas down.
- interrupt.
- monopolize the discussion.
- consider only your point-of-view.
- criticize others.
- call anyone names.

If your teen violates one of these rules, simply remind him with a firm, calm comment: "We agreed that we wouldn't criticize each other, right?" Once you establish ground rules for your family talks, it will be easier to keep everyone in a positive frame of mind.

Family Council Meetings

The highest level of family participation and Active Parenting skills come together in the family council meeting. The family council meeting encompasses family talks, active problem-solving, and many other skills. It is an excellent forum in which all family members solve problems and make family decisions.

A family council meeting is to a family what a business meeting is to an organization. Typically, it is held once a week and lasts from twenty minutes to an hour. It is conducted according to an agenda.

Family council meetings may be the most challenging of all the Active Parenting skills to use because most families struggle to fit family council meetings into their schedules. It may be hard to find a regular time each week to hold a meeting, but you need to make the effort. No other forum allows this much valuable communication among family members.

The Basics of Family Council Meetings

- **Who should attend family meetings?** Anyone who has a stake in decisions affecting the daily life of the family should be present, including anyone who lives with the family, such as grandparents, uncles, or aunts. If you're a single parent, be sure to avoid discussing any problems the children have with the absent parent. These are not your problems to solve. Address them through active communication at another time.

- **What if a family member doesn't want to attend?** Hold the meeting anyway, without that person. He may see later that he is missing out on helping to make important family decisions (many of which will probably affect him).

- **Agree on a time and a place.** Sunday afternoons or right after Sunday dinner make good times, since the family is more likely to be together at these times. It's an opportunity to review the past week and look forward to the upcoming week. The dinner table is a great place for a meeting, since everyone has a chair.

- **The first family meeting should be a short one.** Try addressing only one issue at this meeting, and plan something fun to do right after the meeting. Later meetings can be longer and follow a more extensive agenda, but the first one is more of a practice.

Leadership Roles

Two people need to be leaders at family meetings:

Every family member should take a turn in a leadership role.

- the chairperson, who keeps the discussion on track and sees that everybody's opinion is heard
- the secretary, who takes notes during the meeting and reads the notes at the next meeting

You can perform these two tasks at the first meeting. After that, other family members should take turns so that no one person is in charge every time.

Overall Agenda

Some families think a formal agenda is too businesslike. However, the following structure helps make the meeting a little more special and keeps the process on track.

1. **Compliments.** Family members start the meeting by saying "thank you" for anything that happened last week, if that's appropriate, and by complimenting each other to encourage improvement in behavior. Beginning on this positive note sets a cooperative tone for the meeting.

2. **Reading the minutes.** Last week's secretary reads aloud the notes from the previous meeting.

3. **Old business/new business.** Discuss any unfinished topics from the last meeting and address what's on the agenda.

(4.) **Chores and allowances.** You may choose to discuss family money issues now. Some families pass out allowances at this time.

(5.) **Treat or family activity.** After the meeting ends, stay together for a game, an outing, or a dessert. This time together helps you have fun, enjoy each other's company, and get the week off to a good start.

New Business Agenda

Most families find that the new business section of the family meeting works better when all items are written on a posted agenda before the meeting. A sheet of paper labeled "Agenda" can be taped to the refrigerator or posted at another convenient location. When a problem occurs that a family member would like handled at the next family meeting, she can write it on the agenda.

Example:

Agenda

1. Megan comes into my room without knocking (Ty)
2. Raising allowances (Megan)
3. Planning for the holidays (Mom)

Agenda items that don't get covered in the meeting can be rolled over into the next one. Often family members will solve a problem among themselves before the meeting, so that problem can be dropped from the list.

A written agenda offers parents an excellent way to stay out of their children's fights. When a teen tries to engage you in solving one of his problems, you can sympathetically suggest that he put it on the agenda for that week's meeting.

Example:

Ty: "Megan keeps coming into my room without knocking. Tell her to stop."

Mother: "You sound pretty angry about that. Why don't you put it on the agenda for this week's family meeting?"

The ground rules for handling this type of problem during a family council meeting are exactly the same as those of a problem-solving discussion. When there are no pressing problems on the new business agenda, you may choose to use this time for a family talk.

Drugs, Sexuality, and Violence: More Prevention Strategies

In the past five chapters, we covered half of the ten prevention strategies for reducing your teen's risk of involvement with drugs, sexuality, or violence:

1. Be a positive role model and teacher of values.
2. Educate your teens about the risks of drugs, sexuality, and violence.
3. Establish clear guidelines for behavior.
4. Provide healthy opportunities for challenge.
5. Consult with your teen about how to resist peer pressure.

Let's look now at the remaining five.

6. Monitor and supervise teen behavior.
7. Work with other parents.
8. Identify and confront the use of tobacco, alcohol, and other drugs.
9. Calmly manage a crisis should one occur.
10. Manage your own feelings.

Ten Prevention Strategies for Parents:

Strategy #6. Monitor and supervise teen behavior.

I heard a tragic story about a fight that broke out at a party between teens from two rival high schools. There had been a lot of beer drinking, and everyone was feeling pretty macho. During the fight, one of the teens pulled a knife and stabbed another, who died on the way to the hospital. This took place in an affluent suburb of a typical American city.

You may expect that the parents of the house were out of town, as is often the case with teen parties. They were not. In fact, they were upstairs watching TV. When asked why they were not downstairs supervising the party, they answered, *"Because we didn't want to get in the way."*

Their response is not that unusual. The irony, however, is that it is part of our job as parents to get in the way. We must be willing and able to provide safe limits to our children's freedom until they become capable of establishing these on their own. Research clearly shows that positive parental involvement is a key factor in preventing delinquency, drug use, school failure, pregnancy, and crime. Although it is unwise to try to monitor every moment of a teenager's day, teens who have a great deal of unsupervised time are at a much higher risk for drifting into problem peer groups and developing problems themselves.

Know where your children and teens are, and with whom. As they demonstrate responsibility in handling unstructured time, you can gradually relax your supervision. Even in families in which both parents work outside the home, telephone check-ins can help parents monitor behavior. In addition to knowing where your teen is going in her free time and with whom, it is important to have

It's important to monitor and supervise your teenager, which means being awake when she comes home at night.

agreed-upon curfews. Sit down with your teen and together agree upon guidelines. This is a good way to reduce later conflicts and misunderstandings.

Be awake when your teen comes home to make sure she is following the guidelines. If she does a good job of keeping to the agreed-upon limits, her responsibilities should earn her greater freedom. Likewise, if the guidelines are violated, then logical consequences can be used to reduce freedom.

Ten Prevention Strategies for Parents:

Strategy #7. Work with other parents.

Teens have a tremendous support group—their peers—to back up their behavior. They instinctively understand the principle of power in numbers. Parents can also utilize this principle by forming parent support groups in the community. These "parent networks," as they are often called, can help parents agree on certain issues such as chaperoning, curfews, the need for regular communication among parents, and the unacceptability of alcohol and other drugs being used by children and teens.

Napoleon observed that, "People do not want liberty; they want equality." This is particularly true of teens. Parents know the feeling of an uphill battle when they hear the age-old retort, "But everyone else is . . ." How much easier it is for the teen to give up something he wants when none of the other teens is being allowed to do it either. If your teen's school doesn't not already have a parent's network, use an Active Parenting group to begin one. Talk to your school counselor, psychologist, or social worker about how you can get a group going.

Ten Prevention Strategies for Parents:

Strategy #8. Identify and confront the use of tobacco, alcohol, and other drugs.

Possession of drugs or drug-related paraphernalia is a strong sign that your teen is using.

We talked about the importance of establishing a no-use rule in your family. This is a good starting place. But, for any rule to be effective, the parent must be willing to expend the energy to detect when it has been violated. One of the best ways to determine whether children or teens are using alcohol or other drugs is to notice their behavior when they come in at night. Do they act incoherent or odd? Do you smell alcohol on their breath? Are their pupils dilated? Three signs almost always mean that your child is becoming involved with drugs:

1. possession of drug-related paraphernalia such as pipes, rolling papers, small decongestant bottles, or small butane lighters
2. possession of drugs themselves or evidence of drugs (peculiar plants, butts, seeds, or leaves in ashtrays or clothing pockets)
3. the odor of alcohol or other drugs or the smell of incense or other cover-up scents

Other signs are not conclusive in themselves, but a combination of several of the following usually means that your teen is not only around alcohol or other drugs, but is actually using them:

- heavy identification with the drug culture (drug-related magazines and music, slogans on clothing, conversations and jokes that are preoccupied with drugs, hostility when discussing drugs)

- signs of physical deterioration (memory lapses, short attention span, difficulty in concentration, poor physical coordination, slurred or incoherent speech, unhealthy appearance, indifference to hygiene and grooming, bloodshot eyes, dilated pupils). Again, some of these things are often harmless characteristics of the teenage years, but when many of these appear together, it's time to suspect alcohol or other drug use.

- dramatic changes in school performance: a distinct downward turn in your child's grades (not just from C's to F's, but also from A's to B's to C's), more and more uncompleted assignments, and increased absenteeism or tardiness

- changes in behavior such as chronic dishonesty (lying, stealing, and cheating); trouble with the police; changes in friends; evasiveness in talking about new friends; possession of large amounts of money; increasing and inappropriate anger, hostility, irritability, and secretiveness; reduced motivation, energy, self-discipline, and self-esteem; a diminished interest in extracurricular activities and hobbies

Although all of these symptoms have been found to be associated with alcohol and other drug use, you should not draw conclusions on the basis of one or two of them. Look for an overall pattern of behavior.

In any discussion of detection, parents always ask whether they should search a teen's room. I believe we should show our children and teenagers the same respect that the law, in general, shows us. A police officer may not come into your home and go through your belongings without probable cause and a search warrant; similarly, we ought not to make a routine habit of searching our children's belongings. However, if you have reasonable grounds to believe that a teen is harmfully involved with alcohol or other drugs, I do believe you have the right to go through the teen's belongings in search of hard evidence with which to confront him.

Consider that it is almost impossible to find out whether a teenager is involved with alcohol or other drugs by asking. By becoming involved, the teenager has already made a decision to lie. He will therefore say "no" whether he is using or not. As a last resort, the availability of drug screening through hospitals, labs, drug treatment centers, and at-home urine-collecting kits can offer you a way to clarify whether or not you teen is using drugs. However, drug-testing is not a substitute for any prevention strategy.

Confronting Your Teen

The earlier a drug problem is found and faced, the easier it is to overcome.

Parents frequently deny evidence of drug use and postpone confronting their teen. *The earlier a drug problem is found and faced, the easier it is to overcome.*

If you suspect your teen of using alcohol or other drugs, you must first deal with your own anger, resentment, and guilt. Do not take your teen's alcohol or other drug use as a sign that you are a bad parent. Remember that parenting is not the only influence on a child's development.

When you confront your teen, it's natural to get angry and want to punish him, but this may drive your teen further into alcohol and other drugs. A firm, calm approach works best.

Do not try to have a confrontation while your teen is under the influence of the drug. If your teen is unconscious or semi-conscious, take him immediately to a detoxification center or a hospital emergency room. Do not make the mistake of allowing your child to "sleep it off." In addition to the medical importance of seeking treatment, it also sends your child the clear message that drug use is serious business and is not going to be taken lightly.

Be careful not to react with rage or excessive anger. Although you may feel justified in becoming angry, a calm, firm reaction produces the best results. Trying to embarrass or humiliate your teen is also likely to be counterproductive. Bribery does not work, either. The teen will take the rewards, but continue to use alcohol or other drugs. Threats and unreasonable discipline also tend to drive the teen further into alcohol or other drug use.

Again, the discipline that works best is the use of active problem-solving with logical consequences—the same skills recommended for other violations of guidelines and limits. The key is to be firm, calm, and caring. When we confront out of caring ("I'm doing this because I care about you"), our teens are much more likely to respond positively.

Remember to act more and talk less. Our lectures almost always fall on deaf ears when a teen is already involved in alcohol or other drugs. Following through on logical consequences that you both had agreed upon will capture your teen's attention.

It is essential that you and your partner present a unified front, as any disagreement between the two of you will be exploited by your teen.

If you are married, agree with your partner about how to handle the situation. *It is essential that you present a unified front, as any disagreement between the two of you will be exploited by your teen.* Sit down with your partner and plan how you will confront your teen. A single parent may want to ask an adult friend or relative to assist in the confrontation. You may find strength in numbers. Review the evidence you have found and decide how to present the information in a respectful, yet forceful, manner. It is important that you back up each accusation with examples and evidence.

Think about your goals for the confrontation. If your teen is already in the addicted or heavy-use stage, your goal will be to get her into a treatment program. Consult your local mental health center, a physician, or a hospital that specializes in alcohol or other drug use. Also ask your teen, since he or she still has a choice in the matter. If your teen appears to be in the early stages of drug use, your goal might be to obtain an agreement to cease all use. If you are not sure how far along she is—which is often the case—your goal may be to get her to go for an evaluation, where a professional can help you make the determination. Again, the easy availability of drug screening can help you monitor your teen's future use.

Suicide Threats

Be prepared for your teen to try to divert you from focusing on his drug use. Teens also tend to lie or make excuses or threats when confronted. They may threaten to run away, to behave even more inappropriately, or even to commit suicide. Take any threats seriously, but do not allow yourself to be blackmailed. It is particularly important to treat a suicide threat seriously. Teenager suicide is on the rise. Contact a crisis center, suicide hotline, or mental health center immediately. They can help you assess the situation and determine if the suicide threat is serious or just manipulative. Do not try to make this determination yourself.

Ten Prevention Strategies for Parents:

Strategy #9. Calmly manage a crisis should one occur.

Whether the crisis is a drug overdose, a suicide attempt, pregnancy, or the discovery that your teen has committed a crime or been the victim of one, your calm handling of the situation can make all the difference. Keep the following issues in mind as you manage the crisis.

First, stay calm. Do not blow up or give up. A crisis is not the end of the world, just a larger, more pressing problem. Flying into a rage because your teen has violated your values may drive a wedge between the two of you that may never be removed. Instead, recognize that teens make mistakes, and that your teen needs your support now more than ever. You can discuss differences in beliefs after the crisis has been handled.

Many people are not aware of the many resources available in every community and for every budget. Professionals are available immediately by phone (hot lines), while others are skilled at helping resolve crisises after the immediate danger has passed. Many of these resources are listed in Appendix D of this book. You can find others by calling your pediatrician or a local mental health center, or by searching through your local yellow pages.

Again, do not let an intoxicated teen "sleep it off." This is risky for two reasons. First, teens often drink while using other drugs; your teen may have had a potentially lethal dose of something in addition to alcohol. Even if not, alcohol poisoning itself is a major threat and has killed many unsuspecting teens. If your teen is unconscious or semiconscious, take him to the emergency room of a hospital.

Ten Prevention Strategies for Parents:

Strategy #10. Manage your own feelings.

We've already talked about the importance of staying calm. Be aware that you may feel overwhelming guilt if your teen reaches a crisis. You may have made mistakes in your parenting (we all have), but remember that it is your teen who is ultimately responsible for her choices. Feeling guilty will only make it harder for you to handle the situation effectively.

A more useful feeling is "resolve." Resolve that you will do what you can to handle the problem effectively and to learn from the experience, so you can help prevent such problems in the future. It helps to remember that although you are the most important influence in your teen's life, you are not the only influence.

Letting Go

In the beginning of this book, I stated that the purpose of parenting is to protect and prepare our teens to survive and thrive in the kind of society in which they will live. Preparing your teens for a life independent of you is essential to Active Parenting. In fact, as important a job as effective parenting is to the future of any society, it is also one of the few jobs in which the goal is to work yourself out of a job.

It's been suggested that the most difficult task for any teenager is to break away from his parents and eventually return to them as a fellow adult. The skills presented in this book can help set the stage for such a passage. But it will take one more thing: your willingness to let go.

I have used the image of a ship at sea to describe the voyage your teen will take as she leaves the safe harbors of her family for ports unknown. I've spoken of the storms and icebergs she will encounter, and how you can help give her the kind of character she will need to stay stable in spite of these threats to her safety. Yet, even with the skills you are developing to help prepare her for a safe voyage, it takes courage for you to let go of the rudder and trust that she has what she needs to make the journey.

The concluding poem is my hope that you will have that necessary courage when the time comes to wish your teen "bon voyage."

A Final Gift: Letting Go

(to a Teen Leaving Home)

Boats in the harbor are safe near shore
far from the unknown sea,
But just as boats were made for more,
It's the same with you and me.

Those who would anchor their teens with a stone
In hopes of preventing a wreck,
Find that their fears are never undone
And the stone ends up weighting *both* necks.

So I give to you a port called home
Where your ship was built so strong,
And if you need to harbor here,
You know that you belong.

And I give to you the maps you'll need
That you may set the course
For places that I'll never see,
So go without remorse.

Tilting your sails into the wind
With hope, and vision and courage—
I kiss you once, then touch your chin
And wish you bon voyage!

—Michael H. Popkin

The Active Parenting of Teens Video-Based Program

The following practice sheets are to be used in conjunction with the *Active Parenting of Teens* video, which is a component of the *Active Parenting of Teens* video and discussion program. This program is a six-session parenting education course offered on a local level to parents and other caretakers of teens.

Attending the course offers a variety of benefits, including:

- video vignettes which model positive parenting practices and those you should avoid
- discussion of Active Parenting skills and theory with the group leader and other group members
- discussion of parenting issues in general with other parents, plus their support and guidance
- participation in exercises that demonstrate skills (these are fun!)

To participate in a course, contact your local school system, religious organization, hospital or mental health center, or other "helping professional" in your community. If you are interested in starting your own Active Parenting course, or if you would like to order additional copies of this book (quantity discounts available) call us at 800-825-0060. We'll be glad to guide you with help and resources as you strengthen parenting skills in your home, community, and school system.

Turning Discouragement to Encouragement Video Practice

As you watch the following video scenes during your *Active Parenting of Teens* course, put yourself in your teen's place.

What would you probably . . .

	think	feel	do
Scene 1. How Discouraging: Choosing Friends (Jose and Mother)			
Scene 2. How Encouraging: Choosing Friends (Jose and Mother)			
Scene 3. How Discouraging: The Report Card (Patrice and Father)			
Scene 4. How Encouraging: The Report Card (Patrice and Father)			

(There are no "correct" answers to this exercise!)

Who Owns the Problem
Video Practice

	Who owns the problem?	Why?
Scene 1.		
Scene 2.		
Scene 3.		
Scene 4.		

(Answers on page 237.)

Logical Consequences Video Practice

For each situation, determine which of the eight guidelines (listed on page 151) the parent failed to use. Then write a logical consequence you might use with your teen in a similar situation. The correct answers plus examples of correct logical consequences are on page 238.

	guideline missed	better logical consequence
Scene 1.		
Scene 2.		
Scene 3.		

Responding to Feelings Video Practice

As you watch the following vignettes during your *Active Parenting of Teens* course, identify the teen's feeling in each of examples, write that feeling down in one or two words, and then write down a response you might use to connect this feeling to what happened. Examples of correct answers are on page 239.

teen	feeling word	parent's response
1. Jackie		
2. José		
3. Patrice		
4. Kyle		
5. Roderick		
6. Jennifer		
7. Josh		

Appendix B

Answer Keys

Who Owns the Problem Video Practice Answer Key

	Who owns the problem?	Why?
Scene 1.	Jackie and Andew	Their goal of watching TV is blocked and their relationship is affected.
Scene 2.	Mother	Her goal of having Roderick home on time is blocked.
Scene 3.	Father	His goal of keeping his son drug free is at issue.
Scene 4.	It's shared.	The teen has a responsibility to go to school, and the parent has a responsibility to see that she does.

Logical Consequences Video Practice Answer Key

	guideline missed	possible logical consequence
Scene 1.	Mother did not give a choice, and the consequence was not logically connected to the problem behavior.	"Patrice, you can either pick up after yourself, or I'll be your personal maid and pick up after you—at the rate of $1 a minute."
Scene 2.	Mother's tone of voice is so angry it invites a power struggle; withholding guitar lessons as a consequence is not logically related to the gas problem; and Mother does not involve the teen in solving the problem.	"Kyle, either put gas in my car when you use it or find yourself some other transportation next time."
Scene 3.	This consequence is not logically connected to the misbehavior; Mother doesn't include her son in deciding the consequence.	"You can be home on time or the next time, I'll come over to the court and get you."

Responding to Feelings Video Practice Answer Key

scene #	feeling word	parent's response
1. Jackie	worried	You seem worried about the kids on the bus.
2. José	excited	That's great! How exciting!
3. Patrice	frustrated	You sound really frustrated.
4. Kyle	disappointed	Oh. I know how disappointed you are.
5. Roderick	bored	You seem bored.
6. Jennifer	angry	You're really angry at him.
7. Josh	embarrassed	You sound embarrassed.

(Please remember that there are others answers that work here too.)

Connecting Feelings to Content Answer Key

Mother: Hey. You seem pretty miserable. You've never skipped school before.

Jarret: Well, I'm not going so don't even try.

Mother: You sound pretty angry about it.

Jarret: You would be too.

Mother: I see. What happened to get you so upset?

Jarret: Nothing.

Mother: Sometimes it helps to talk about it.

Jarret: I doubt it . . . and it's not going to make me change my mind about going.

Mother: Well, I can't make you go, Jarret. And I don't know what you're gonna decide to do, but I would like to talk to you about it.

Jarret: Well, Steve, he's a senior and the editor of the yearbook and I'm on the staff for the ninth grade and he called this big meeting and started yelling about people missing deadlines and the only person he called out by name was me . . .

Mother: Oh Jarret, that must have really hurt.

Jarret: I wanted to crawl under a desk and die.

Mother: Pretty embarrassing!

Jarret: Exactly. I've never been so humiliated. I just can't go back there!

Mother: I can see why you'd feel that way.

Jarret: You can?

Mother: Sure. I can remember . . . well, maybe I shouldn't tell you this.

Jarret: Come on! I told you . . .

Mother: Well, okay . . . See I was already a senior, and I went to the movies with a date and we parked. All we did was kiss a little, well he told everyone I was really easy and implied we'd done a lot more . . .

Jarret: Uhg! What a jerk.

Mother: Believe me, I called him worse when I found out, but it was incredibly embarrassing what happened.

Jarret: Well, what can I do? I can't call him a jerk. Besides, I have missed some deadlines.

Mother: I see. So as your editor he has the right to expect you to handle your responsibilities.

Jarret: I guess . . . But he didn't have to yell at me in front of everyone!

Mother: No, I agree. That was uncalled for. Well, let's look at your options. You can hang out here with me the rest of your life.

Jarret: Ugh. No offense.

Mother: None taken. Okay, so what else could you do?

Jarret: I could just quit the yearbook. Write him a note or something.

Mother: You could quit. But how would that make you feel?

Jarret: Like a quitter.

Mother: Doesn't sound like you, anyway. Tell me something—is this Steve guy really a bad guy or was he maybe just feeling the pressures of deadlines himself?

Jarret: Both. He's yelled at other people before.

Mother: I see. Well, there's something you need to know about the world of work. Some bosses are like that, and you have to decide whether you want to work with them or go someplace else. Of course, when you miss deadlines, you get fired, too.

Jarret: Yeah, well it's not that bad. I mean he does compliment me on my work, sometimes.

Mother: What if you asked to talk to him and told him how you felt about what happened?

Jarret: Well . . .

Mother: I know. It would take a lot of courage.

Jarret: Well, I'll think about it.

Mother: Well, let me know how it goes.

Appendix C
Drug Chart

Drug	Trade or Street Names	Appearance	Method of Use	Psychological Effects	Physical Effects	Withdrawal Symptoms
Narcotics						
Codeine	often abused through Tylenol with Codeine, Empirin Compound, and cough medicines with codeine.	dark, thick liquid, tablets, or capsules	swallowed or injected	immediate rush, then tranquil and euphoric effect	breathing, heart rate, and brain activity slow	diarrhea, abdominal cramps, chills, sweating, nausea, insomnia, etc. Sleeplessness and craving can last for several months after abruptly stopping use.
Heroin	dope, H, junk, smack, horse (heroin and cocaine combined is speed balling)	white to dark brown powder or tar-like substance	injecting, snorting, smoking			
organic methoxies	Dexedrine, Methedrine, Meperidine, Pethidine, Demerol, Mepergan, Cylert, Tenuate, Fastin, Preludin; 'drines, lightweight speed	white powder, liquid, tablets	swallowed or injected			
Other narcotics	Percocet, Percodan, Tussionex, Fentanyl, Darvon, Talwin, Lomotil, Dilaudid, Morphine, Demerol, Methadone	Tablets, capsules, liquid				
Stimulants						
Amphetamines	Biphetamine, Delcobese, Desoxyn, Dexedrine, Benzedrine, Mediatric; speed, uppers, dexies, crystal, crank, yellow jackets, No Doz	pills, powder	swallowed, snorted, injected	users feel restless, moody, anxious, and talkative, with a sense of self-confidence or superiority.	reduces appetite, increases breathing and heart rate, raises blood pressure, dilates pupils. Higher doses causes fever, blurred vision, dizziness, diarrhea, constipation, rapid and irregular heartbeat, tremors, loss of coordination or physical collapse. Prolonged use can lead to malnutrition, skin disorders, ulcers, depression, and psychosis.	fatigue, irritability, intense hunger, moderate to severe depression
Cocaine/Freebase/ Crack	coke, snow, nose candy, blow, white, lines/rock	white powder or powdery rocks/light brown pellet of powder	snorted, injected/ smoked	initial euphoria, increased energy, alertness, self-esteem, and sensory awareness. After the high users will feel irritable and agitated, craving the drug again.		violent, erratic, paranoid behavior, anxiety, hallucinations, nausea, sleep disorders, severe depression, muscle aches, and intense craving
Nicotine	in cigarettes, pipes/smokeless tobacco	chemical in tobacco	smoked/ chewed	initial feeling of well-being, then psychological stress	increases heart rate and blood pressure, decreases appetite and urine production, tremors, quickened breathing; cancer of the mouth, larynx, pharynx, esophagus, lungs, pancreas, cervix, uterus, and bladder; heart disease, colds, gastric ulcers, chronic bronchitis, stroke, emphysema, blood clots	changes in body temperature, heart rate, digestion, muscle tone, and appetite. Irritability, anxiety, sleep disturbances, nervousness, headaches, fatigue, nausea, and a craving for tobacco.
Depressants						
Alcohol	(many common names)	liquid	swallowed	Initial boost of self-confidence and energy, followed by sleepiness and depression	slurred speech, disorientation, shallow respiration, clammy skin, dilated pupils, weak and rapid pulse. Overdose can bring coma and possible death	anxiety, insomnia, tremors, delirium, convulsions, cravings, possible death
Barbiturates	Phenobarbital, Tuinal, Amytal, Nembutal, Seconal, Lotusate; barbs, red, downers, sopors	capsules, tablets, powder	injected, swallowed	disorientation, depression	cold and clammy skin, dilated pupils, shallow respiration, weak and rapid pulse, possible coma and/or death	convulsions, toxic psychosis

Drug	Trade or Street Names	Appearance	Method of Use	Psychological Effects	Physical Effects	Withdrawal Symptoms
Benzodiazepines (tranquilizers)	Ativan, Azene, Buspar, Clanopin, Dalmane, Diazepam, Halcion, Lacion, Librium, Meprospan, Paxipam, Restoril, Serax, Tranxene, Valium, Valrelease; Verstran, Xanax	capsules, tablets, powder	injected, swallowed	disorientation, depression	cold and clammy skin, dilated pupils, shallow respiration, weak and rapid pulse, possible coma and/or death	convulsions, toxic psychosis
Other depressants	Chloral Hydrate, Methaquatone (Quaaludes)					

Hallucinogens

Drug	Trade or Street Names	Appearance	Method of Use	Psychological Effects	Physical Effects	Withdrawal Symptoms
Marijuana/ Hashish	pot, weed, reefer, ganja, grass, sinsemilla/hash	stems, leaves, and buds from green or brown plants/solid, black resin	smoked/eaten in foods	distortion of sensory perception, especially vision and sense of time. Sometimes includes panic reactions.	elevated heart and pulse rates, bloodshot eyes, dry mouth and throat, impaired short-term memory, slowed thinking and reflexes. Long-term use includes: difficulty understanding complex ideas and concentrating, loss of memory, irregular sleep, mood swings, decrease in muscle strength, sinusitis, bronchitis, lung cancer, reproductive problems in men and women	psychological dependence, insomnia, and irritability.
LSD (Lysergic Acid Diethylamide)	acid, trips, blotter, microdot, windowpane, tabs	liquid in an eye dropper or on small squares of paper or other tiny edible items	swallowed	distorted sense of distance and time, estrangement, illusions, hallucinations	dilated pupils, higher body temperature, increased heart and blood pressure, sweating, loss of appetite, sleeplessness, possible back-ache	none
PCP (Phencyclidine)	angel dust, hog, loveboat	white or yellowish-white powder, tablet or capsule	swallowed, injected, smoked with marijuana	disassociation from reality, distorted sense of distance and time, estrangement, illusions, hallucinations	sedation, numbness, dizziness, loss of coordination, decreased blood pressure, breathing, heart rate, confused speech, distorted vision. High doses can cause seizure and coma. Severe disorientation causes most PCP injuries and deaths. Dilated pupils, higher body temperature, increased heart and blood pressure, sweating, loss of appetite, sleeplessness	unknown
Mescaline and Peyote	mesc, buttons, cactus	hard, brown discs, tablets, capsules	eaten or smoked	similar to LSD	similar to LSD	none
Psilocybin	'shrooms, mushrooms, magic mushrooms	dried, brown mushrooms	eaten or steeped in water for tea			

Other Drugs

Drug	Trade or Street Names	Appearance	Method of Use	Psychological Effects	Physical Effects	Withdrawal Symptoms
Designer drugs (synthetic versions of PCP, heroin, Demerol, amphetamines and meth-amphetamines)	TCP, PCE, PCPY, PCC, wack, space base, china white, MPPP, PEPAP, glass, MDMA (ecstacy or X), MMDA, DMA, DMMM, 2CB, para-DOT	all forms	smoked, swallowed, injected	similar to the original drugs each is a copy of.	similar to original drug	similar to original drug
Steroids	steroids	liquid/pills	injected/ swallowed	initial euphoria, followed by increased irritability and inappropriate displays of anger, with potential depression, paranoia, suicidal tendencies	increased development of bone, muscle, skin, hair, lower voice, acne, possible enlargement of prostrate, prostrate cancer, stunted growth, heart attack, stroke, baldness, shrinking of testicles or breasts or uterus, reduced sperm production or irregular menstrual cycles	unknown
Inhalants	solvents, glue, ether, laughing gas, whippets, nitrous, rush, poppers	gas is in canisters or balloons or rises from solvents	sniffed or inhaled or sprayed into the nose or mouth	at low doses, users feel stimulated; at moderate amounts, they feel light-headed, less in control. At high amounts, users lose consciousness.	slows down the body's functions. May cause weight loss, fatigue, electrolyte imbalance, damage to nervous system, bone marrow, the liver and kidney damage. Can slow breathing down until it stops. Causes headaches.	none

243

Hotline Numbers for Parents and/or Teens

Alcohol and Other Drugs

Al-Anon/Alateen Family Group Headquarters, Inc.: 800-356-9996. Resources for family members of alcoholics and teen alcoholics.

Alcohol and Drug Helpline: 800-821-4357. Referrals to local alcohol and drug-dependency units and self-help groups.

Alcoholics Anonymous World Services: check the phone directory for your local AA chapter or call 212-870-3400.

American Council for Drug Education: 800-488-DRUG

Center for Substance Abuse Treatment (C-SAT) National Drug Hotline: 800-662-4357. Confidential information on drug or alcohol abuse and related issues. Referrals to local drug treatment centers and counseling centers. Sponsored by Center for Substance Abuse Treatment, Drug Information Treatment, and Referral Hotline.

Cocaine Hotline: 800-COCAINE: 800-262-2463. Information and referral service for drug and alcohol addiction and treatment. Sponsored by National Medical Enterprises.

Nar-Anon Family Group Headquarters, Inc.: 310-547-5800 for family members of narcotics abusers.

National Clearinghouse for Alcohol and Drug Information: 800-729-NOTO (Mon-Fri, 8am-7pm EST). Information on alcohol and drug abuse, prevention, drugs and crime, treatment centers, research, groups, drugs in the work place, community programs, AIDS and drug abuse, and criminal justice and drugs. www.health.org

National Council on Alcohol and Drug Dependency: 800-622-2255. Refers calls to counseling and treatment centers for alcohol and drug abuse.

Community Resources

Community Anti-Drug Coalitions of America: 800-DRUGS-50 for information on current issues or legislation.

Just Say No International: 800-258-2766 for community-based drug prevention.

National Job Corps Information Line (bi-lingual): 800-733-5627 (Mon-Fri, 8:30am-6:30pm EST). Referrals to job corps training (persons 16-24). Sponsored by National Job Corps Alumni Association.

Crisis Intervention

Boy's Town National Hotline: 800-448-3000. Provides short-term crisis intervention, information, and referrals for general population. Free, confidential. Works with children and families.

KID SAVE: 800-543-7283. Information and referrals to public and private services for children and adolescents in crisis. Referrals to: shelters, mental health services, sexual abuse treatment, substance abuse, family counseling, residential care, adoption/foster care, etc.

NineLine: 800-999-9999. Referrals for youth or parents regarding drugs, homelessness, runaways, etc. Message relays, reports of abuse. Helps parents with problems with their children. If all counselors are busy, stay on line and one will be with you as soon as possible. Sponsored by Nine Line/Covenant House.

Eating Disorders

America Anorexia/Bulimia Association, Inc.: 212-575-6200

National Association of Anorexia Nervosa and Associated Disorders: 847-831-3438

Miscellaneous

Juvenile Justice Clearinghouse: 800-638-8736 (Mon-Fri, 8:30am-7pm). Information and referrals regarding juvenile justice programs and department of justice. www.ncjrs.org

Parents and Friends of Lesbian and Gays (PFLAG): 202-638-4200 PFLAGNTL@aol.com

National AIDS Hotline: 800-342-AIDS; Spanish: 800-344-7432 (8am-2am EST); Deaf: 800-AID-7889 (Mon-Fri, 10am-10pm EST); Teens: 800-234-TEEN. Answers basic questions about AIDS/HIV (prevention, transmission, testing, health care). Referrals and free literature. Sponsored by American Social Health Association.

National Family Violence Hotline: 800-222-2000. Provides a taped message with information only. Sponsored by the National Council on Child Abuse and Family Violence.

National STD Hotline: 800-227-8922 (Mon-Fri, 8am-11pm EST). Education, research and public policy about sexually-transmitted diseases. Information on minor and major STDs. Referrals, information on prevention, free pamphlets.

Mental Health

National Foundation for Depressive Illness: 800-248-4344. Recorded message has information on the signs of depression and manic-depression.

National Clearinghouse Family Support/Children's Mental Health: 800-628-1696. Leave message and you will receive either a return call or written information. Sponsored by Portland State University.

SAFE (Self-Abuse Finally Ends): 800-DONT-CUT. Referrals to local programs dealing with self-abuse and self-mutilation.

Suicide Crisis Center: 214-828-1000

Pregnancy

Planned Parenthood: 800-829-7732 (Mon-Fri, 8:30am-5pm) provides family services for planned parenthood with offices throughout the country.

Pregnancy Hotline: 800-848-5683. Free, confidential information for pregnant women, shelters for girls, baby clothes, adoption referrals.

Pregnancy Hotline: 800-238-4269. Information and counseling to pregnant women. Referrals to free pregnancy test facilities, foster and adoption centers. Sponsored by Bethany Christian Services.

Runaways

Child Find Hotline: 800-I-AM-LOST (Mon-Fri, 9am-5pm EST). Helps parents to locate children. Helps lost children who need assistance. Sponsored by Child Find.

Missing Children Help Center/Kidsrights: 800-872-5437. Advises parents of missing children.

National Center for Missing and Exploited Children: 800-843-5678. Information on missing and exploited youth. Helps parents to locate missing children.

National Runaway Switchboard: 800-621-4000. Information and referrals for runaways regarding shelter, counseling, food pantries, transportation. Suicide and crisis counseling.

Vanished Children Alliance: 800-VANISHED directs victims to help. Conducts investigations, sends out photos, provides educational training and materials. Offers technical assistance and disseminates information.

Youth Crisis Hotline: 800-HIT-HOME. Crisis hotline and information and referral for runaways or youth with other problems and their parents. Sponsored by Youth Development International.

This is a partial list of available services. Active Parenting Publishers does not recommend or endorse any specific organization or hotline number service.

References

Books

Adler, Alfred. *The Practice and Theory of Individual Psychology.* New York: Harcourt, Brace, 1920.

Albert, Linda and Michael Popkin. *Quality Parenting.* New York: Random House, 1989.

Ansbacher, H. L. and R. Ansbacher. *The Individual Psychology of Alfred Adler.* New York: Harper Torchbooks, 1964.

Bernal, M. E., and G. P. Knight. *Ethnic Identity: Formation and Transmission among Hispanics and Other Minorities.* Albany: State University of New York Press, 1993.

DeLong, Mark R. and Webb C. Howell, eds. *Full Potential: A Guide for Parents of Bright Teens.* Durham: Tag Books, 1995.

Dinkmeyer, Don and G. McKay. *Systematic Training for Effective Parenting.* Circle Pines, MN: American Guidance Service, 1976.

Driekers, Rudolf, and V. Stolz. *Children: The Challenge.* Des Moines: Meredith Press, 1964.

Ellis, A. *Reason and Emotion in Psychotherapy.* New York: Lyle Stuart, 1962.

Fine, M. *The Second Handbook on Parent Education.* San Diego: Academic Press, 1989.

Ginott, Haim. *Between Parent and Child.* New York: MacMillan, 1965.

———. Haim. *Between Parent and Teen.* New York: MacMillan, 1969.

Gordon, Thomas. *Parent Effectiveness Training.* New York: Peter H. Wyden, 1970.

Hartmann, Thom. *Attention Deficit Disorder: A Different Perception.* Lancaster, PA: Underwood-Miller, 1993.

Helms, J. E., ed. *Black and White Racial Identity: Theory, Research, and Practice.* New York: Greenwood Press, 1990.

McCoy, Kathleen. *Coping with Teenage Depression: A Parent's Guide.* New York: NAI Books, 1982.

Pipher, Mary. *Reviving Ophelia: Saving the Selves of Adolescent Girls.* New York: Ballantine Books, 1994.

Ponterotto, J. G., et al. *Handbook of Multicultural Counseling.* Thousand Oaks: Sage Publications, 1995.

Popkin, Michael H. *Active Parenting of Teens Parent's Guide.* Atlanta, GA: Active Parenting Publishers, 1990.

———. *Active Parenting: Teaching Cooperation, Courage and Responsibility.* New York: HarperCollins, 1987.

———. *Active Parenting Today Parent's Guide.* Atlanta, GA: Active Parenting Publishers, 1992.

Schroeder, Beverly Allred. *Human Growth and Development.* St. Paul: West Publishing Company, 1992.

Waldman, Larry. *Coping with Your Adolescent.* Norfolk: Hampton Roads Publishing Company, 1994.

Articles

"20 Ways We've Changed," *MotherJones.* www.bsd.mojones.com/motherjones/JF96/anniversary/20ways.html. (Accessed 2 June 1997).

American Psychiatric Association Joint Commission on Public Affairs and the Division of Public Affairs. *Teen Suicide,* Internet Health Resources Company. www.psych.org/publicinfo/TEENAS~1.HTM. 9 January 1996.

Apfel, Ira. "Teen Violence: Real or Imagined?" *American Demographics,* June 1994. www.marketingtools.com/publications/AD/95_AD/9506_AD/AD7558B.HTM. (Accessed 9 July 1997).

Bennett, William. "Sex and Education of Our Children," U.S. Department of Education. Transcript of talk at the National School Board Association, 22 January 1987. Quoted in McDowell, Josh. *Myths of Sex Education.* San Bernadino, CA: Here's Life Publishers, 1990.

Borden, Sally and Karen Shue. "Teen Dating Violence," SAVE (Shelter Against Violent Environments). www.infolane.com/save/teen.html. (Accessed 2 June 1997).

"CDC: Tobacco Industry to Blame for Teen Smoking," Health, *USA Today.* 7 August 1996.

Elium, Don and Jeanne Elium. "When a Son says He's Gay," Parent Soup. www.parentsoup.com/library/docs/dk1050.html. (Accessed 7 July 1997).

"Dispelling Myths about Alcohol." 198.115.232.254/Y2Y/dispelling_myths.html. 6 September 1994.

Farley, Dixie. "On the Teen Scene: Eating Disorders Require Medical Attention," *FDA Consumer,* March 1992. www.fda.gov/opacom/catalog/eatdis.html. (Accessed 7 July 1997).

Futrelle, David. "Sex and the Single Girls: Shotgun Marriages, Perp-Hunts and 'Family Values' Are Not the Answer," *Salon Magazine.* www.salon1999.com/news/news960909.html. (Accessed 22 July 1997).

Gushue, G. V. "Cultural Identity Development and Family Assessment: An Interaction Model." *The Counseling Psychologist* 21 (1993) 487-513.

Loftus, Mary J. "Confronting our Counterculture Past: Baby boomers who dabbled in drugs when they were younger, now wonder what to say if their children ask about it," *The Gainseville Sun,* 13 October 1996.

Long, Philip W. "Marijuana: Facts for Teens," National Institute on Drug Abuse, U.S. Department of Health and Human Services," NIH Publication No. 95-4037. Internet Mental Health. www.mentalhealth.com/book/p45-mari.html. 1 March 1997.

McCoy, Kathleen. "A New Look at Boy-Crazy Girls," parentsplace.com.www.tnpc.com/parentalk/adolescence/teens17.html. 24 October 1995.

———. "Who Is at Risk for Eating Disorders," www.parentsplace.com. 1995.

Mathias, Robert. "Studies Show Cognitive Impairments Linger in Heavy Marijuana Users." *NIDA Notes* 11, no. 3 (1996).

"Marijuana Sends Teens to Emergency Rooms," Health, *USA Today.* 8 July 1996.

Milne, Carly. "Violence 101: Scared at School," *Spank.* Laughing Dog Publications. www.spankmag.com/foc/foc.9htm. (Accessed 5 May 1997).

"Parent's Chemical Use Self Test." www.childplace.com/uul3.htm. (Accessed 2 June 1997).

Peterson, Karen S. "Teens Unlikely to Talk about Depression," Health, *USA Today.* 8 July 1996.

Rocco, Susan. "For Teens Only: Balancing Lifestyle Changes," *Families . . . Priority—1.* The Ohio State University Extension. www.ag.ohio-state.edu/ohioline/hyg-fact/5000/5230.html. 21 May 1997.

Schoemer, Karen. "Rockers, Models and the New Allure of Heroin," Lifestyle, *Newsweek.* 26 August 1996.

"Study: Teen Drug Use Rises," News Release, Clarinet e.News!. 206.61.184.43/schaffer/Other/teenuse.htm. 15 December 1995.

Sylvester, Kathleen. "What to Do with Those Teenage Mothers." *The Washington Post,* 7 August 1995.

Szapocznik, J., and Kurtines, W. M. "Family Psychology and Cultural Diversity." *American Psychologist* 48 (1993): 400-407.

"Teen Pregnancy Bill: $29B," Health, *USA Today.* 7 August 1996.

"The Hidden World of Dating Violence," *Parade Magazine.* 22 September 1996.

Viscio, Randolf Louis. "Juvenile 'Justice': Over Six Million Served," *As We Are.* Cambridge. www.vineyard.net/awa/issue3/Juvenile_Justice.html. 8 October 1995.

Vogler, Roger E. and Wayne R. Bartz. *Teenagers and Alcohol: When Saying No Isn't Enough.* Philadelphia: Charles Press, 1992.

Wibbelsman, Charles. "How to Help Your Teen's Body Image," parentsplace.com. 24 October 1995. www.tnpc.com/parentalk/adolescence/teens22.html.

Research Reports

Center for Disease Control and Prevention. *Youth Risk Behavior Surveillance—United States,* 1993. Department of Health and Human Services. Healthy People 200: National Health Promotion and Disease Prevention Objectives. DHHS Publication No. 91-50212. Washington, DC: U.S. Government Printing Office, 1990.

Center for Disease Control and Prevention. *Youth Risk Behavior Surveillance—United States, 1993. Morbidity and Mortality Weekly Report* 44 (1995):1-56.

"Facts about Marijuana and Marijuana Abuse," *NIDA Notes* 11, no. 2 (1996).

"New National Poll on Kid's Health and Safety," Children Now/Kaiser Permanente, childrennow.org/health/poll_summary.html. 12 October 1996.

Office of National AIDS Policy. "Youth & HIV/AIDS: An American Agenda: A Report to the President." www.thebody.com/onap/fullrpt.html. 5 March 1996.

U.S. Department of Health and Human Services, Substance Abuse and Mental Health Services Administration, Office of Applied Studies. *Historical Estimates from the Drug Abuse Warning Network,* Advance Report No. 16. August 1996.

U.S. Department of Health and Human Services, Substance Abuse and Mental Health Services Administration, Office of Applied Studies. *Preliminary Estimates from the Drug Abuse Warning Network: 1995 Preliminary Estimates of Drug-Related Emergency Department Episodes,* Advance Report No. 17. August 1996.

U.S. Department of Health and Human Services, Substance Abuse and Mental Health Services Administration, Office of Applied Studies. *Preliminary Estimates from the 1995 National Household Survey on Drug Abuse*, Advance Report No. 18, August 1996.

U.S. Senate Committee on the Judiciary. *Losing Ground against Drugs: A Report on Increasing Illicit Drug Use and National Drug Policy.* 19 December 1995.

Valencia Community College Project Infusion Module, Orlando, FL. 1992.

Notes for pages 38–39

[1] U.S. Department of Health and Human Services, *1995 National Household Survey.*

[2] DeLong and Howell, *Full Potential.*

[3] U.S. Department of Health and Human Services, *1995 National Household Survey.*

[4] Ibid.

[5] Loftus, "Confronting our Counterculture Past."

[6] Center for Disease Control and Prevention, *Youth Risk Behavior Surveillance.*

[7] Peterson, "Teens Unlikely to Talk about Depression."

[8] Futrelle, "Sex and the Single Girls."

[9] Department of Health and Human Services, Healthy People 2000.

[10] Office of National AIDS Policy, "Youth & HIV/AIDS."

[11] Apfel, "Teen Violence."

[12] "New National Poll on Kid's Health and Safety."

[13] Borden and Shue, "Teen Dating Violence."

[14] Viscio, "Juvenile 'Justice.'"

[15] Ibid.

Additional Violence Resources

Books

Levine, Madeline. *Viewing Violence: How Media Violence Affects Your Child's and Adolescent's Development.* New York: Doubleday, 1996.

Sachs, Steven L. *Street Gang Awareness: A Resource Guide for Parents and Professionals.* Minneapolis: Fairview Press, 1997.

Videos

Big Changes, Big Choices: Preventing Conflicts and Violence, Michael Pritchard, 1994. 30 mins., includes Discussion Guide.

Kids Killing Kids, AIMS Multimedia. 58 mins.

Peace Talks, Michael Pritchard, 1997. 30 mins., includes Leader's Guide.

Tragic Consequences: Teenagers and Guns. United Learning, 1995. 48 mins., includes Teacher's Guide and blackline masters. (Also available in Spanish.)

Violence, Power Surge Videos, 1995. 15 mins., includes lesson plan and two homework projects.

Violent Times: Straight Talk II, Attainment Company, 1996. Three videos, 25 mins. each.

Violence Prevention: Inside Out. United Learning, 1993. 63 mins., includes Resource Guide.

Working it out at Madison: Working it Out, Not Just Anybody, Breaking the Chain, and Tough Cries, Forefront Productions, 1993. Four videos, 25 mins. each, includes Leader's Guide.

Notes:_____